Flash Floyd

Flash Floyd

timeless favourites
from around the world

Keith Floyd

CASSELL
ILLUSTRATED

First published in Great Britain in 2002 by Cassell Illustrated,

a division of Octopus Publishing Group Limited

2-4 Heron Quays, London E14 4JP

Location photographs: Kim Sayer

Food photography: Michelle Garrett

Editor: Barbara Dixon

Designer: Mark Stevens

Keith Floyd is represented by Stan Green Management, Dartmouth, Devon;

telephone 01803 770046; fax 01803 770075; e-mail sgm@clara.co.uk

visit www.keithfloyd.co.uk

A CIP catalogue record for this book is available from the British Library.

ISBN 1 84403 008 3

Printed in Hong Kong

Contents

Introduction

There are two questions that I am repeatedly asked. One is, what is your favourite meal, and the other is, since you eat all that wonderful food (how do they know!), how do you keep so slim?

On the subject of eating gorgeous food, it is true that over the last forty-odd years I have probably spent more time in restaurants, bars and hotels than my liver or my wallet could reasonably stand. I am not, in fact, a glutton, nor do I live exclusively on a diet of quails' eggs stuffed with larks' tongues delicately flavoured with a truffle sauce! (By the way, you will find this recipe in my next book, which will be entitled *Why I am not a 3 star Michelin Chef*, to be published in the spring of 2004!) And, although food, cooking and drinking is a passion of mine, it is not an obsession, nor is it my only passion and I am as happy to eat a shepherd's pie with a dollop of baked beans as I am to drool over Lobster with a rhubarb and ginger Chardonnay sauce prepared by Alain Ducasse in his exquisite restaurant in Monte Carlo.

My interest in food developed at an early age. My mother was an excellent cook and my father a keen gardener and, since we lived in the country in Somerset, my sister and I were despatched, depending on the time of year, to pick wild fruits for jam and watercress from the stream for watercress sandwiches for Sunday teas, and autumn would find us tromping the misty fields collecting mushrooms. We lived next door to my grandfather, who was the village cobbler, and often farmers would pay for his services in kind so there were always tubs of rich, yellow clotted cream, legs of home-cured ham and gorgeous curls of salty, farmhouse butter. My father also kept chickens, both for eggs and to eat, and my uncle, who was something of a poacher, often took me with him on his rambling trips and we would return with a pheasant, a hare or a brace of rabbits. I also helped supplement the larder with fresh rainbow trout, perch or eels from my fishing trips. Even my grandfather, who had a tin leg as a result of First World War injuries, occasionally turned his hand to the pot. Saturdays he would boil pigs' trotters and we would eat them, drenched with salt and vinegar, with our fingers, seated around the fire on Saturday nights. Sometimes, after a heavy summer shower - and I can still smell the rain on the privet hedge that surrounded our garden - my grandfather would collect snails (I presume he cleansed them properly!) and he would cook them on the coal shovel over the fire. Then, with pins, we would pick them out of their shells and, as with the pigs' trotters, splash them with salt and vinegar. Occasionally, when there was a glut of tomatoes, he would infuriate my grandmother by commandeering the kitchen, then create absolute mayhem but, leaving the place littered with pots, ladles, spoons and sieves, would produce the most amazing tomato ketchup.

The travelling fishmonger came to the village once a week, so Fridays we had the most wonderful cod and chips and, or, poached cod with parsley sauce, and Saturday and Sundays there were treats of grilled kippers and smoked haddock, but the greatest treat of all was the occasional special Sunday breakfast of slabs of poached, salted cod served with oodles of butter and freshly baked bread that I would collect from the Golden Hill Bakery in Wivelliscombe.

From the age of 12, I was encouraged - actually I was forced - to get some kind of job during the school holidays, so I got a job as an odd-job boy in the local hotel where I would wash up or peel potatoes, weed the vegetable garden or bottle up the bar, and I suppose I continued, unwittingly, as I watched the owner's wife cook, to absorb more and more understanding of food.

I think I was 17 or 18 when I experienced a gastronomic sea change that was to influence me to this very day. I was taken to the legendary Hole in the Wall Restaurant in Bath where the great George Perry-Smith was the chef/patron. There I ate for the first time in my life such delicacies as ratatouille, French country terrine, moules marinière, partridge stewed with cabbage, white wine and juniper berries, and a creamy gratin of thinly sliced potatoes (which I ate with a brimming glass of Gevrais Chambertin). At the end of the meal I asked Mr Perry-Smith how he had acquired his culinary skills. 'It is quite simple, dear boy,' he said, 'I just follow Elizabeth David's recipes!' Next payday, I bought a paperback version of Elizabeth David's *French Country Cooking* and, as a consequence, I have been cooking and eating beyond my means ever since!

Central to being a good cook, along with an understanding of how to eat, is to know how to shop, and I am a consummate, although perhaps reckless and extravagant, shopper, especially when it comes to food and wine. As much as I enjoy an evening at the theatre, or an afternoon on the touchline of any rugby pitch anywhere, or as much as I dream of landing a big salmon, or as I sit on the banks of some tranquil, sun-dappled canal fishing for carp or tench, I still get a huge thrill visiting the market, be it in Provence, Tuscany, Bangkok, Sydney, Naples, Saigon, Kerala, Barcelona, Stockholm, Singapore, Cape Town, Prague, Vienna, Madagascar, London, Malacca, Istanbul, Athens, Cairo or Marrakesh. Although I must admit, I felt a bit sick in a market in Hong Kong where I watched merchants plucking live chickens or, indeed, in Singapore, where once you have chosen your live frog, they rip off the legs and throw the tortured carcass into a bin. And you do have to shield your eyes in Vietnam at the cages of snakes, dogs, squirrels and bats waiting for the pot.

Whilst filming in the Arctic Circle I got into terrible trouble with a misguided press for cooking a puffin. On this particular flat, bleak island the only way to avoid killing a puffin was not to walk on the ground. The place was covered in the ruddy things and once a year, to maintain a centuries' old tradition, the locals catch a couple and cook them. They taste like wild duck, jolly nice too!

Another time I found myself in trouble (by the way, this book does not have enough pages to recount every such occasion) while I was shopping in Tesco's in Didcot. We don't come to England very often and do occasionally have a yen to stock up the English section of our larder as some of the exotica is hard to find in the Med. For example, gravy granules, Heinz spaghetti, baked beans, macaroni cheese and tomato soup, Shiphams fish paste, Sarsons malt vinegar, salad cream, Roses lime cordial and marmalade, HP sauce, poppadoms, tinned salmon, tinned pilchards, corned beef and all! I was recognised at the checkout by some frightfully smart old dear who stared into my trolley and shrieked with scorn and disbelief that she was shocked that I had a trolley full of what she considered to be junk food, and told me she would never watch my programmes again! However, the checkout lady was very nice and asked for my autograph. You win some, you lose some. Anyway I really like baked beans on toast and cheddar cheese with Branston Pickle.

These days, my approach to cooking is very simple and straightforward. No matter where I find myself in the world, I head for the nearest market and then, entirely on whim, buy a selection of ingredients. Because I am usually cooking in impossible situations – for example, once I roasted a leg of lamb in a wood-fired oven made of sheets of metal and slabs of turf in Greenland, in Madagascar I cooked on a charcoal grill made from a car wheel, and in Zambia I baked custard cream in a hole in the ground on a banana plantation – I have to be very, very organized. I always have a selection of bowls or plastic trays so that everything that needs to be peeled or chopped, skinned or deseeded is prepared long before I begin to cook. So, when a recipe says 'first sauté your onions' make sure that you have them already prepared and chopped up. Also, remember, at the end of the day, that cooking is simply a question of applying raw food to a source of heat. I love entertaining people, but I don't do 'dinner parties'. I think too many people, particularly in Britain, put themselves under too much stress by attempting to prepare an over-complicated, four-course dinner party, not to mention about six different vegetables, when they are much better off cooking just a couple of dishes that do not stretch the resources of their kitchen. The classic occasion is Christmas – it is just not possible in the average domestic kitchen to roast a turkey, roast the potatoes, roast the parsnips and stuffing and maintain your sanity. And when you do give a dinner party, your guests are getting legless in the sitting room while you are frantically trying to work out how you can get your soufflé into the oven at the same time as you are trying to lightly sear some steaks of tuna fish which are wrapped in Parma ham, to be served with a light ginger and raspberry dressing. All the while, your colourful iced mousse of spring vegetables hasn't set, no-one has bothered to bring you out a glass of wine, and you suddenly realise that you absolutely hate your guests and wish you'd taken them to the local Chinese instead. Then, just as you are about to turn the page of the glossy cookbook you were given for your birthday, the cat jumps onto the table and splatters the crème fraîche all over the beautiful photograph that encouraged you to this culinary madness in the first place.

For heaven's sakes, having friends around is meant to be fun for everybody and especially you. After all, you have paid for it, and anyway, when you do eventually manage to get the food onto the table, all they are going to do is talk about a wonderful meal they had in their favourite restaurant or tell you that their particular favourite TV cook wouldn't have done it like that.

No. Take the heat out of the kitchen – stay simple, stay fresh, stay fast, which is just what the recipes in this book are designed for. And you could be a bit flash and take advantage of the good ready-made wine sauces, stocks, etc. that are available in supermarkets – after all, we're all busy people nowadays.

Oh yes! How do I stay so slim? I don't eat pompous four-course dinners. Oh, and the other question was, what is my favourite meal? Well, if you can be bothered to read on, you will find about 100 of them!

Best dishes and happy cooking.

KEITH FLOYD

Soups, Light Meals, Salads and Snacks, and Vegetable Dishes

The nature of my job means I have to travel a huge amount and seldom a week goes by when I am not on a plane, in a train or a car heading for some exotic or indeed, from time to time, mundane destination. As a consequence I spend several months a year staying in hotels of varying degrees of luxury. After a while, the predictability and the strictures of hotel food begin to get you down and as sure as hell airline food is about the most depressing in the world.

On a brighter note I am very fortunate to be entertained in fine restaurants around the world by advertising agencies, PR companies and the like and I know many, many people would give their right arm to share my globetrotting, exotic lifestyle. When we go off on a long trip we pack a trunk that we call 'the really useful box' with some emergency supplies and rations, so that every now and again we can have an illicit picnic in our hotel suite. The box always contains a small electric ring, a little camping gaz stove (by the way I buy the gas locally), a frying pan, saucepan, kettle etc., and lots of sachets of strong instant coffee, tea bags, Tabasco, Worcestershire sauce, brown sauce, tomato sauce, English mustard, Marmite and gravy granules, to name but a few. Not to mention first aid kit, sewing kit, world-band radio, a framed photo of the cat and dog and a load of books to read. So, when we get home we tend to be absolutely foodied out and so we cook quick, simple and quite light little meals like the ones that follow (though I must admit the Country Terrine and the Italian Fish Soup take a bit longer than the majority of the recipes, but they were too good to leave out).

Thai prawn soup

This delightfully refreshing, tangy, clear soup is a kind of all-purpose Asian soup.

This particular dish I adapted after a visit to Thailand.

Total preparation/cooking time: 45 minutes
Serves 4

225g/8oz raw prawns, deveined, shells removed and
    reserved, but tails left intact
450ml/¾pt rich chicken stock
2.5cm/1in piece fresh root ginger, coarsely chopped
2–3 stalks lemon grass, chopped
4 Kaffir lime leaves, fresh or dried
60ml/2fl oz fish sauce
60ml/2fl oz lime juice
a few ounces of fresh (preferably exotic) mushrooms,
    finely sliced
3 green chillies, deseeded and chopped
2 shallots, finely chopped
2 cloves garlic, finely chopped
a few slivers of fresh coconut
1 tbsp chopped fresh coriander and/or basil leaves

1 Put the chicken stock into a large pan, add the prawn shells, which will give the soup extra flavour, the ginger, lemon grass and lime leaves, bring to the boil and simmer for 20 minutes. Strain the stock. Return the stock to a pan and add the fish sauce, lime juice and a little cold water.

2 Bring to the boil and add the mushrooms, chillies, shallots, garlic and coconut slivers. Cook gently for around 3 minutes, until the prawns turn pink. Serve garnished with coriander and/or basil leaves.

Thai prawn soup – hot and sour flavours, with ginger, mushrooms and chilli

Provençale fish soup

For this superb soup, which can be a meal in itself, you need a selection of small Mediterranean fish. You will see them advertised in French markets and fish shops either as *poissons de roche* or a *soupe de poissons*. You will need about a kilo of this. If you can't find it, use such things as small gurnard, red mullet, soft-shelled crabs, red snapper, etc., etc. All need to be gutted, scaled and de-finned, then chopped into fairly small pieces.

Total preparation/cooking time: 45 minutes
Serves 4

1kg/2¼lb mixed fish, gutted, descaled, de-finned and
    chopped into fairly small pieces
olive oil
4 large ripe tomatoes, roughly chopped
1 leek with green part, chopped
1 onion, finely diced
chopped fresh fennel fronds or 1 small fennel bulb,
    finely diced
1 large stick celery with its leaves, chopped
1 large carrot, finely diced
4 garlic cloves, very finely chopped
a large pinch saffron strands
sea salt and freshly ground black pepper

For the aïoli
10 garlic cloves, peeled
2 egg yolks
1 egg
about 300ml/½pt olive oil
lemon juice

To serve
thin rounds of baguette, fried on both sides in olive oil
finely grated Parmesan cheese (optional)

1 To make a quick aioli, purée the garlic in a food processor, then add the egg yolks and whole egg and whiz until well amalgamated. With the motor still running, slowly pour in enough olive oil to make a thick mayonnaise. Season with lemon juice, salt and pepper. Keep in the fridge until required.

2 Heat the olive oil in a pan and fry the tomatoes, leek, onion, fennel, celery, carrot and garlic until soft. Add the fish and about 1.7 litres/3pts of water, bring quickly to the boil, then turn down to a simmer. When the fish is cooked, ladle the lot into a food processor and blend. Then strain it through a fine sieve into another saucepan, pushing it through the sieve with a spoon so that all the fleshy bits go through but not the bones and things. Reheat the soup very gently then add the saffron and season with salt and pepper.

3 To serve, spread the warm baguette slices with aïoli and float them in the bowls of soup, then sprinkle on the Parmesan cheese, if using.

Mussel chowder

This is a rich, creamy, thick soup. It can be adapted to use clams or scallops or indeed any firm white fish, such as monkfish.

Total preparation/cooking time: 50 minutes
Serves 4

3kg/6½ lb mussels in shells
4 sprigs fresh thyme
1 bunch fresh parsley, leaves finely chopped, stalks
     coarsely chopped
2 bay leaves
1 tsp black peppercorns, plus extra to serve
1 bottle dry white wine
butter
3 onions, finely chopped
1 leek, diced
2 carrots, finely diced
4 garlic cloves, chopped
6 peeled potatoes, cut into small cubes
450ml/¾pt double cream
1 tsp ground turmeric, or some saffron if you can
     afford it
freshly ground coriander seeds

1 Wash and scrub the mussels thoroughly in cold water, and remove beards and barnacles. Discard any that are open. Heat a large pan and add the mussels, thyme, parsley stalks, bay leaves and peppercorns and about a third of the wine. Cover and cook until the mussels have opened. Discard any that don't open. Pour the contents of the pan through a conical sieve and reserve the juices. Leave about 16 of the mussels in their shells, and of the remainder leave half whole and chop the rest (without shells).

2 Heat a little butter in a pan and sweat the onions, leeks, carrots and garlic until softened. Add the rest of the wine and the stock from the mussels. Bring to the boil, add the potatoes and cook until they are tender. Add the whole and chopped mussels and most of the cream and heat through. Add the turmeric or saffron, then pour into individual bowls.

3 Garnish each bowl with a few mussels in their shells, some chopped parsley and a dollop of cream. Offer your guests either freshly ground coriander seeds or black peppercorns to sprinkle into the soup.

Chilled gazpacho

Total preparation time: 30 minutes
**This amount will be enough for about
    10–12 people**

1 litre/1¾pts natural, pure tomato sauce, with no
    additives
10 cloves garlic, peeled and chopped
2kg/4½lb tomatoes, skinned, deseeded and finely
    chopped
ice cubes
olive oil
wine vinegar
4 tbsp sugar
1kg/2¼lb total weight of finely chopped onions, peeled
    and deseeded cucumber, and chopped red peppers
    in equal quantities
a handful of fresh tarragon leaves
sea salt and freshly ground black pepper

Basically a tomato soup, gazpacho can be puréed till smooth and drunk from a glass like a Bloody Mary, or it can be left coarse and lumpy and eaten from a bowl. I like both versions, but this is my recipe for the chunky one. It keeps very well in the fridge.

1 Put the tomato sauce, garlic, half the tomatoes and a load of ice cubes into a large food processor. Add about ½ cup of olive oil and ½ cup of wine vinegar and whiz until the ice has broken down and you have a lovely cold soup. Taste it to see if it needs a little more oil or vinegar.

2 Add the sugar and plenty of salt and pepper and, if it's a bit too thick, whiz in some more ice cubes. Now add the remaining chopped vegetables and the tarragon and serve very cold. Nothing in this dish is cooked.

Thai chicken soup

Total preparation/cooking time: 25 minutes
Serves 4

225g/8oz boned and skinned free-range chicken breast,
    very thinly sliced
400ml/14fl oz rich chicken stock
1 tbsp very thin strips fresh root ginger
3 stalks lemon grass, chopped
4–5 Kaffir lime leaves or curry leaves, coarsely chopped
125ml/4fl oz lime juice
4 tbsp fish sauce
1 tbsp brown sugar
480ml/16fl oz coconut milk
2 tbsp chopped fresh coriander leaves
5 green or red chillies, deseeded and finely chopped

The coconut milk in this recipe takes some of the fire out of the chillies so don't be tempted to reduce their number – they give the soup an authentic Thai taste.

1 Put the stock, ginger, lemon grass and lime or curry leaves into a large pan and bring to the boil. Add the chicken, lime juice, fish sauce and sugar and simmer for a few minutes, then add the coconut milk and simmer until the chicken slices are tender, about 5-10 minutes.

2 Serve the soup sprinkled with the coriander and chillies.

Thai chicken soup - coconut milk, ginger and lemon grass combine superbly in this tasty soup

Purée of salt cod (brandade)

A purée of salt cod will be found all over the Mediterranean. In Provence it is often served as part of the Christmas Eve celebrations. It is usually served on country bread fried in olive oil or sometimes in light, pastry vol au vent cases. Or it is put into a flat dish, covered with a creamy purée of potatoes, covered in grated cheese and grilled, rather like a fishy shepherd's pie! If you decide to serve it, say in a vol au vent case or on a nice croûton, make a crunchy salad with a few sweet tomatoes to go with it.

**Total preparation/cooking time: 20 minutes
    plus soaking
Serves 4 as a main course, 8 as a starter**

800g/1¾lb thick fillet of salt cod
6–10 garlic cloves, peeled
600ml/1pt milk
300–400ml/10–14fl oz extra-virgin olive oil
juice of 1 lemon
grated nutmeg
thin slices of country bread, fried in olive oil, to serve

1 The day before preparing the purée, soak the salt cod in changes of fresh, cold water for 24 hours. The next day, rinse the fish and cut it into large chunks. Place the pieces in a saucepan with the garlic, cover with milk and simmer gently for about 20 minutes until the fish is cooked. Drain the fish and reserve the cooking liquid and garlic. Flake the fish, discarding the skin and bones.

2 Warm the olive oil in a pan. Put the fish and garlic into a food processor and blend for a few seconds. Add the lemon juice and nutmeg and then alternately pour in the still-warm milk and the olive oil until you have a smooth purée. Serve as above.

Tartare of game fish with rosti potato

I had never eaten char, a member of the salmon and trout family, until I had spent a day ice fishing in the Arctic Circle. The locals there tend to bury this fine fish in the ground until it stinks like hell and they then eat it raw on bizarre festive occasions. I couldn't face that so I decided to create this dish for my hosts in Finmark.

Total preparation/cooking time: 12 minutes plus marinating
Serves 4

about 700g/1½lb fillets of very, very fresh char, trout or salmon
1 tub crème fraîche
110g/4oz lumpfish roe or any caviar, such as salmon or sturgeon

Lime and ginger marinade
finely grated zest and juice of 2 limes
150ml/¼pt groundnut oil
2.5cm/1in piece fresh root ginger, peeled and finely chopped
pinch of salt
pinch of sugar
1 red chilli, deseeded and finely chopped

Rosti potato
3 large potatoes
1 onion
110g/4oz clarified butter, melted
salt and freshly ground black pepper
fresh dill or parsley sprigs, to garnish

1 Chill the fish fillets in the freezer for 30 minutes before slicing. In the meantime, mix together all the ingredients for the marinade.

2 Slice the chilled fish as thinly as possible into 7.5cm/3in lengths. Put the fish strips into the marinade, cover and leave for an hour.

3 Meanwhile, make the rosti. Grate the potatoes and the onion quite finely, mix with 2 tbsp of the butter, season well with salt and pepper and form into rounds about 1cm/½in thick. Heat the remaining clarified butter in a pan and fry the rosti for about 4–5 minutes, until golden brown on both sides.

4 Place the rosti in the centre of your serving plates and coat them with some crème fraîche. Layer the fish elegantly on the rosti. Spoon some marinade over the fish, place a dollop of crème fraîche on top of the fish, add the caviar and sprinkle on the fresh herbs.

An Italian fish soup – a splendid
lunch dish

An Italian fish soup

This makes a jolly good lunch dish, and one that you feel inspired to make after an exhilarating stroll around a busy fish market on a warm summer's day. It is not worth making this soup for less than six people.

Total preparation/cooking time: 1¼ hours
Serves 6–8

2kg/4½lb firm-fleshed fish, filleted and cut into large
    pieces (choose from a mixture of eels, monkfish,
    squid, clams, octopus, scampi tails, etc.)
90ml/3fl oz olive oil
2 sticks celery, finely chopped
1 small onion, finely chopped
1 small carrot, finely diced
1kg/2¼lb ripe plum tomatoes, skinned, deseeded and
    chopped
3–4 anchovy fillets, chopped
1 tbsp each chopped fresh basil and parsley
2–3 cloves garlic, finely chopped
1.4 litres/2½pts hot water
salt and freshly ground black pepper
chopped fresh basil and parsley, to garnish

1 Heat the olive oil in a very large saucepan and sauté the celery, onion and carrot for a few minutes until they are softened. Add the tomatoes and anchovies and cook until the tomatoes are well melted. Keep stirring so that nothing sticks then add the basil, parsley and garlic. Season with salt and pepper. Pour in the hot water and bring to the boil.

2 If you are using octopus or squid, pop this into the pan, turn the heat down and simmer for about 15-20 minutes before adding the rest of the fish, then cook gently for about 20 minutes more.

3 Ladle the stew into warmed bowls and garnish with the basil and parsley.

Finger-lickin' mussels

These spicy mussels couldn't be simpler to prepare and they're dead good! I bought a large bowl of them from a floating kitchen as I was paddling around the Bangkok Floating Market many moons ago.

Total preparation/cooking time: 25 minutes
Serves 2–3

700g/1½lb mussels in shells
3 tbsp groundnut oil
3 shallots, finely chopped
3 cloves garlic, finely chopped
1 tbsp soy bean paste
1 red chilli, deseeded and chopped
2.5cm/1in piece fresh root ginger, chopped
1 tsp brown sugar

1 Wash and scrub the mussels thoroughly in cold water, and remove beards and barnacles. Discard any that are open.

2 Heat the oil in a large pan and lightly brown the shallots and garlic. Then add the chilli and ginger, and then the mussels and soy bean paste and cook over a high heat for a minute or so before adding the sugar.

3 Cover the pan and cook over a high heat for about 5 minutes, shaking the pan frequently until the mussels have opened and released their juices. Give a quick stir so that all the ingredients are well mixed.

4 Discard any mussels that haven't opened. Serve the mussels in bowls and eat with your fingers. Delicious!

Finger-lickin' mussels –
they're dead good!

Moules à la marinière

Despite the magic of modern cooking, this still remains high on the list of classic, but simple, dishes.

Total preparation/cooking time: 20 minutes
Serves 6

1.5kg/5lb black, shiny mussels
a very generous knob of butter
8 cloves garlic, finely chopped
2 shallots, finely chopped
1 bottle of the best dry white wine you can afford
1 small bunch parsley, finely chopped
1 bouquet garni (thyme, bay leaf and tarragon)
freshly ground black pepper

1 Wash and scrub the mussels thoroughly in cold water, and remove beards and barnacles. Discard any that are open. Melt half the butter in a large pan, add the garlic and shallots and cook for 2-3 minutes, or until they are shiny. Now add the mussels, wine, half the parsley and the bouquet garni. Cover the pan and cook over a high heat, shaking the pan from time to time until the mussels have opened.

2 Remove the mussels to a serving dish and boil the liquid to reduce it a little. Stir in the remaining butter and pour the liquid back over the mussels in the serving dish. Discard any mussels that haven't opened. Season generously with freshly ground black pepper, sprinkle on the remaining parsley and serve.

Mussel and spinach gratin

Total preparation/cooking time: 40 minutes
Serves 4–6

Prepare the mussels as for Moules à la Marinière (above) but use only a quarter of a bottle of wine to cook them in. Strain and reserve the cooking liquor and remove all the mussels from their shells. Discard any that are closed.

Next, melt a knob of butter in a pan over a low heat, stir in a tablespoon or two of plain flour, mix well together and cook gently until you have a smooth paste. Add a little of the reserved mussel liquor to create a smooth sauce, whisking all the while. Add a little crème fraîche and season this fish-flavoured béchamel with some salt and pepper. Allow to cool and put to one side (this is really the way you would make a cauliflower cheese).

Next, stir-fry some fresh spinach leaves in a little butter until they are soft, then strain them thoroughly to remove all liquid. Mix the shelled mussels and the spinach together and place them in a gratin dish. Cover with the béchamel sauce, grate some Parmesan or gruyère cheese over the top and pop under the grill. Grill until golden brown, and then serve.

Smoked fish fillets with leek and potato cake

For this little dish you can use buckling, smoked herring, eel or trout etc.

Total preparation/cooking time: 35 minutes
Serves 4

500g/1lb 2oz smoked fish fillets, cut into elegant slices

For the leek and potato cakes
25g/1oz butter
2 leeks, trimmed and finely chopped
500g/1lb 2oz potatoes, cooked and mashed
2 egg yolks
2–3 tbsp double cream
50g/2oz plain flour
olive oil or butter, for frying
salt and freshly ground black pepper

For the apple and beetroot salad
1 red apple, diced
1 medium pickled beetroot, drained and diced
225g/8oz crème fraîche
2 tbsp chopped fresh chives

For the garnish
mixed salad leaves
very finely sliced red onion rings
lemon wedges

1 To make the leek and potato cakes, melt the butter in a frying pan and sauté the leeks for about 5 minutes until softened, but not browned. Mix with the mashed potatoes, egg yolks, cream and seasoning. Shape the mixture into little patties, dust them with flour and fry in olive oil or butter (or a mixture of both) for about 4 minutes each side until golden and crunchy.

2 While they are cooking, mix together the apple, beetroot, crème fraîche and chives to make a salad. Season with salt and pepper.

3 Put the warm potato cakes on serving dishes, scoop the apple and beetroot salad on top and place the smoked fish fillets on top of that. Decorate with a few salad leaves, red onion rings and lemon wedges and splash a drop of olive oil over the lot.

Sweet-and-sour pickled cherries

These sweet-and-sour pickled cherries go really well with the French country terrine opposite. They're also good to nibble on while you're having an aperitif.

Make at least one month in advance; they will keep for up to a month once opened.

Total preparation/cooking time: 25 minutes plus marinating

2.25kg/5lb cherries in perfect condition
sugar for sprinkling
1 litre/2pts white wine vinegar
3 cloves
10 black peppercorns
1 bay leaf
salt

1 Trim the stalks of the cherries, leaving a little protruding from the fruit. Wash and dry the cherries thoroughly, put into preserving jars and sprinkle lightly with sugar.

2 Meanwhile, bring the vinegar to the boil with the cloves, peppercorns and bay leaf. Add a little salt and boil for a further 5 minutes or so. Allow to cool. Pour the liquid over the cherries and seal the jars.

French country terrine

I know it is wonderful to enjoy the superb way in which super chefs create exquisite dishes with foie gras, but I still adore this classic terrine. I serve mine with a bowl of simply dressed green salad or with a dish of crunchy gherkins or some sweet-and-sour pickled cherries (see opposite).

Total preparation/cooking time: 1½ hours
     plus standing and cooling
Serves 4–8

110g/4oz pork fat, cut into 12mm/½in cubes
250g/9oz pig or chicken liver, minced
450g/1lb deskinned belly of pork, finely chopped
350g/12oz shin of veal, minced
2 cloves garlic, finely chopped
shallow tbsp black peppercorns, crushed
2 juniper berries, crushed
1 large glass dry white wine
1 generous splash Armagnac or Cognac
2 eggs, beaten
2 tbsp double cream or crème fraîche
salt and freshly ground black pepper
1 sachet aspic powder

1 Combine all the ingredients except the aspic in a bowl and leave to stand for a couple of hours in a cool place.

2 Preheat the oven to 170°C/325°F/gas mark 3. Tip the mixture into a terrine and place the terrine in a baking tin. Pour enough hot water into the tin to come halfway up the sides of the terrine. Cook for about 1½ hours. To check if it is cooked pierce the terrine with a skewer and if it comes out clean, it is ready. Remove from the oven and allow to cool a little in the terrine.

3 While it is warm, make up the aspic and pour into the terrine, cover with clingfilm and chill for at least 12 hours before serving.

Summer vegetable terrine

The aspic jelly in this terrine seals in all the wonderful flavour of the vegetables.

Total preparation/cooking time: 30 minutes
     plus chilling
Serves 6

2–3 tbsp olive oil
4 red peppers, blanched, peeled, deseeded and sliced
4 courgettes, sliced
3 aubergines, peeled and thinly sliced
10 plum tomatoes, blanched, peeled, deseeded and sliced
1 onion, finely chopped
1 tsp crushed garlic
1 tbsp each fresh chives, coriander, dill and parsley, all
     finely chopped
2 tbsp aspic powder
450ml/¾pt tomato juice

1 Heat the olive oil in a large pan and fry the peppers, courgettes, aubergines, tomatoes, and onion separately in batches with a little garlic. Allow them to cool.

2 Arrange the aubergines in a layer in the bottom of a terrine dish, followed by a layer of the tomatoes. Cover with a layer of the chopped herbs, then add a layer each of the courgettes, peppers and onion.

3 Dissolve the aspic in the tomato juice and then pour this over the vegetables in the dish until covered. Put the lid on and chill for 2-3 hours before serving.

Fresh peas with ham and chicken – the Italian job

Fresh peas are one of the hardest vegetables to cook; not only that, you have to spend hours shelling them and, quite frankly, frozen peas are so good (as are, indeed, the French petits pois *'melange printanier' à l'étuvée* that you can buy in tins) that why bother. In fact, outside of my childhood a million years ago, where my father carefully tended his peas in our little garden and my mother cooked the little sweet green things gently and served them with mint and butter, the only other time I had fresh garden peas that I thoroughly enjoyed was in Alastair Little's restaurant in Soho one hot London day, at least 12 or 14 years ago. That is, however, until I discovered this dish on the little island of Marettimo, an hour or so from the west coast of Sicily.

Total preparation/cooking time: 35 minutes
Serves 4

1kg/2¼lb fresh peas (after shelling)
olive oil
a knob of butter
2 carrots, chopped into small dice
110g/4oz diced prosciutto or parma ham or the
    equivalent of smoked bacon lardons
1 diced chicken breast
1 or 2 wineglasses of dry white wine
1 bunch spring onions, chopped
150ml/¼pt milk
a handful of chopped fresh oregano
salt and freshly ground black pepper

1 Heat the olive oil and butter in a large frying pan. Add the carrots, prosciutto or bacon and the chicken and sauté for 2 or 3 minutes, until softened.

2 Add the wine and bubble it up until it has reduced to half its volume. Then add the peas, spring onions, milk and oregano and season with salt and pepper. Simmer until you have a beautiful dish of tender peas, ham and chicken in what should now be a creamy sauce.

Scandinavian hash

This versatile dish can be made either with fresh ingredients, e.g. small cubes of fillet steak, raw potato and onion, or with cubes of left-over boiled potatoes and cold roast lamb. It also works well with bacon.

Total preparation/cooking time: 20 minutes

For each person
a generous knob of butter
1 small onion, chopped
1 large potato, cut into tiny cubes or a left-over boiled one
1 fillet steak, cut into cubes, or the remains of the Sunday roast, lamb, beef or pork cut into cubes
a dash of Worcestershire sauce (optional)
chopped fresh dill and parsley
salt and freshly ground black pepper
1 free-range egg yolk

1 Melt some of the butter in a heavy frying pan, add the onion and cook until browned. Remove from the pan and set aside. Add some more butter to the pan and cook the potato until browned and tender. Remove from the pan. Add the steak and cook over a high heat for a few moments.

2 Put the onion and potato back into the pan, mix everything together and add a dash of Worcestershire sauce, if using. Season with salt and pepper; then pile onto your plate and scatter the dill and parsley on top and stir in a raw egg yolk.

Potato waffle with caviars and crème fraîche

We're all familiar with sweet waffles, but I came across these savoury ones on my journey to Scandinavia. You often get them served at breakfast time, which is great.

Total preparation/cooking time: 25 minutes plus chilling
Serves 6 or so

250g/9oz self-raising flour
2 eggs
300ml/½ pt milk
120ml/4fl oz single cream
110g/4oz butter, melted
175g/6oz potato, finely grated
vegetable oil for cooking
salt and white pepper

To serve
salad leaves, lightly tossed in olive oil and lemon juice
110g/4oz salmon caviar
110g/4oz red lumpfish roe
110g/4oz black lumpfish roe
300ml/½ pt crème fraîche
1 red onion, finely sliced
6 quail's eggs or 3 hen's eggs, hard-boiled and halved

1 To make the waffle mixture, sift the flour into a large bowl, make a well in the middle and crack the eggs into it. Add the milk, cream and melted butter, and whisk together until you have a smooth batter. Beat in the potato and season well with salt and pepper. The batter should have the consistency of double cream. Cover and chill for 2 hours.

2 To cook the waffles, use a waffle iron, or cook them in some vegetable oil in a small, heavy-based frying pan on both sides until golden brown. Put each waffle on the centre of a plate. Pile some salad leaves onto the middle of each plate, top this with the soured cream, red onion rings and the hard-boiled eggs and then spoon on the caviars. Of course Sevruga would be ideal.

Floyd's Vietnamese spring rolls – little morsels to dip into spicy sauces

Floyd's Vietnamese spring rolls

The finest spring rolls I have ever eaten were in Ho Chi Minh City in Vietnam. They are light and delicate and about the size of your little finger, a long cry from those thick, fat, greasy, floury pancake rolls, stuffed with stale beansprouts that you often find in takeaways and pubs throughout the United Kingdom. The secret is to acquire sheets of pure rice paper, use fresh ingredients and be generous with fresh herbs.

My recipe can work equally well with any combination of chicken, pork, crab, lobster, shrimp, prawns, etc.

A nice thing to do is to have a flower vase filled with bunches of these herbs that make not only an attractive table decoration but you can eat them as well.

Total preparation/cooking time: 20 minutes
Serves 4

For the filling
225g/8oz cooked chicken breast fillet, skinned and very finely chopped or minced
110g/4oz cooked white crabmeat, flaked
1 carrot, finely grated
about 10 spring onions, finely chopped
50g/2oz chopped, cooked rice vermicelli
1 or 2 fresh red or green chillies, very finely chopped (absolutely optional extra)
1 egg, beaten
a quantity of rice paper cut into small rectangles
light corn syrup or a little beaten egg
good-quality nut oil for deep-frying
salt and freshly ground black pepper

To serve
crunchy lettuce leaves
fresh coriander and basil leaves
dipping sauces

1 To make the filling, put the chicken, crabmeat, carrot, spring onions and vermicelli into a bowl. Add the egg and seasoning to taste and mix well together.

2 Dip the rice paper wrappers one at a time into cold water to soften them, and dry well with kitchen towel. Put a spoonful of the filling in the centre of each wrapper then brush one side of each wrapper with the syrup or beaten egg. Foll each wrapper into a finger-shaped tube and press down to seal.

3 Heat the nut oil until hot and deep-fry the rolls for about 5 minutes until they are cooked through, golden and crisp. Turn the rolls during cooking to prevent burning.

4 To eat, pick a leaf of each of the fresh herbs, wrap them tightly round the roll then rip off a piece of lettuce leaf and wrap that around the outside. Dip into a variety of sauces such as soy, fish, sweet and sour, Nuoc Cham or similar.

Satay with peanut sauce

Throughout south-east Asia, street vendors grill these delicate, tiny kebabs over little charcoal barbeques that might resemble a terracotta flowerpot, might be an adapted car wheel or even a little griddle on a tin box on the back of a tricycle. The meat is basically pork, beef or chicken, cut into very small cubes, not much more than half an inch, speared on thin pieces of bamboo or wood only a few inches long, marinated in herbs and spices and coconut milk and then grilled.

If you want to make it in advance, the peanut sauce will keep well for a few days in the fridge.

**Total preparation/cooking time: 20 minutes
   plus marinating
Serves 4–6**

700g/1½lb lean pork, beef or chicken, cut into bite-size
   pieces

For the marinade
2.5cm/1in piece fresh root ginger, finely chopped
4 shallots, finely chopped
2 stalks lemon grass, finely chopped
2 tsp ground coriander seeds
a pinch ground aniseed
a large pinch each ground cumin and ground turmeric
a dash of nut oil
1 tbsp brown sugar
salt

For the peanut sauce
2 red or green chillies, deseeded and finely chopped
2.5cm/1in piece fresh root ginger, finely chopped
6–8 shallots, very finely chopped
2 stalks lemon grass, finely chopped
a dash of nut oil
225g/8oz ground roasted peanuts
2 tbsp sugar, brown or caster
a dash of tamarind juice, or lime or lemon juice
salt

1 To make the marinade, blend all the ingredients into a smooth paste.

2 Thread the pieces of meat onto metal skewers or bamboo sticks. Place in a suitable tray, cover with the marinade and chill for 2 hours.

3 Meanwhile, make the peanut sauce. In a food processor, blend the chillies, ginger, shallots and lemon grass into a purée. Heat the nut oil in a pan and fry the purée for a few minutes, stirring well. Add the remaining ingredients and enough water to loosen the mixture and simmer for a couple of minutes, until the sauce is thick.

4 Grill the satays over charcoal or under a hot grill for about 6–8 minutes, turning and basting during cooking. Serve with the peanut sauce.

Layered Provençal omelette

Many, many years ago, before he set off to work pruning his vines or harvesting his cherries, the Provençale farmer, or indeed farmworker, would breakfast possibly on a slice of country bread, rubbed with a clove of garlic and drenched in olive oil. He might have had a piece of hard goat's cheese or a slice of sausage. While he was eating that, his wife would make a variety of omelettes that he would later eat cold in the shade of an olive tree, washed down with a jug of wine and some grainy country bread. Depending on what was in the store cupboard, she might make a tomato omelette, a courgette omelette and a cheese omelette – each individual omelette cooked in a small omelette pan, placed one on top of the other and then wrapped in a piece of cloth; in a funny way, if you catch the obscurity of my drift, in the same manner that Cornish tin miners went to work with a pasty that contained pilchards or meat at one end and jam at the other. Anyhow, today this dish has been refined by grand masters of the kitchen and they make exquisite thin omelettes, stack them together, press them together in the fridge and cut them into little slices to nibble with their aperitif, as anyone who has visited that brilliant place in Monte Carlo can tell you.

Total preparation/cooking time: 30 minutes plus cooling
Serves 4

olive oil
2 large tomatoes, skinned, deseeded and finely diced
2 decent-sized garlic cloves, finely chopped
1 large courgette, partly peeled, then deseeded and finely chopped
2 shallots, finely diced
8–10 eggs
2 heaped tbsp freshly grated Parmesan cheese
½ cup finely chopped cooked spinach
1 large red pepper, roasted, skinned, deseeded and finely chopped
butter
sea salt and freshly ground black pepper

1 Heat the olive oil and fry the tomatoes briefly with half the garlic and some salt and pepper, then transfer to a plate to cool. Fry the courgette with the remaining garlic in the same way, then place on a separate plate to cool. Fry the shallots in a little olive oil, then season and set aside.

2 Whisk the eggs with a little salt and pepper and a dash of water until frothy, then divide between 5 small bowls or as many bowls as you wish to make omelettes. Then put your tomato mixture into one lot of egg, courgette in the next, Parmesan cheese and shallots in the next, spinach in the next, and red pepper in the next. Mix each one up.

3 Heat some butter and a dash of olive oil in a small omelette pan and set about making the omelettes. Place the first cooked one on a plate, then make the next one and stack it on top of the first. Keep making and stacking until you have a multi-layered omelette cake.

4 Put a plate and a heavy can or something similar on top and leave to cool, then put it in the fridge. Cut into small wedges to serve.

Mediterranean omelette

Leo was a friend of mine who filled this omelette with about 175g/6oz sliced fresh truffle instead of vegetables. I once ate it with him in the hot Provençal sun. But that was in 1987 and Leo, who was the patron of the Café de France, has long since passed on. I include this recipe from *Floyd on France* (1987) in his memory.

Total preparation/cooking time: 25 minutes
Serves 4

olive oil
1 red pepper, deseeded and finely chopped
2 tomatoes, skinned, deseeded and chopped
2 courgettes, thinly sliced
1 large onion, finely chopped
fresh thyme
6 free-range eggs, beaten
salt and freshly ground black pepper

1 Heat the olive oil in a good heavy iron pan about 15-20cm/6-8in in diameter and fry the vegetables until they are translucent. Season with thyme, salt and pepper and put to one side.

2 Clean the pan and heat more oil. Add half the beaten eggs. Once this begins to firm up, pour in the vegetable mixture and cover with the remaining beaten eggs. Cook for about 5 minutes then slide onto a plate and flip back into the pan, uncooked side down. Cook for about another 5 minutes. Eat hot or cold - actually it is better cold.

Indian masala omelette

Unlike Leo's truffle omelette or my Mediterranean omelette (see above), this exquisite Indian breakfast dish is served very thin and is only about 15cm/5-6in in diameter.

Total preparation/cooking time: 15 minutes

Per person
2 large fresh eggs
vegetable oil
1 tsp each finely chopped onion, finely chopped
    tomato, chopped green chilli and chopped fresh
    coriander leaves
salt and freshly ground black pepper

1 Break the eggs into a bowl and whisk thoroughly with some salt and pepper.

2 Heat a little oil in an omelette pan and quickly fry the onion, tomato, chilli and coriander. Pour the beaten egg evenly over the pan and cook until the omelette is set. It should not be more than 12mm/½in thick. Using a spatula, fold the omelette in half and serve at once.

Italian cheese fondue

This superb, delicate and expensive fondue should be served in individual soup bowls, topped with a lightly poached egg, well seasoned with a little salt and black pepper.

Total preparation/cooking time: 15 minutes
Serves 4

600ml/1pt milk
350g/12oz grated Gruyère or similar cheese
4 eggs, beaten
75g/3oz unsalted butter, cut into tiny cubes
2 or 3 white or black truffles, very, very thinly sliced
salt and freshly ground black pepper
4 eggs, freshly poached

1 Heat the milk in a double saucepan, add the cheese and stir until it has amalgamated. Then whisk in the beaten eggs and butter and continue whisking until you have a smooth, creamy consistency.

2 Add the sliced truffles, season with salt and pepper, tip into individual serving bowls and top each one with a poached egg.

Broad bean pesto tart

Total preparation/cooking time: 35 minutes
    plus chilling
Serves 6

1kg/2¼lb fresh broad beans, peeled
1 splash olive oil
1 clove garlic, crushed
juice of 2 lemons
1 sprig mint, coarsely chopped
2 sprigs parsley, coarsely chopped
110g/4oz Parmesan cheese, grated
½ tsp wholegrain mustard
6 tomatoes, skinned, deseeded and chopped
1 tbsp black olives, stoned and chopped
6 individual shortcrust pastry tart cases, cooked

1 Cook the broad beans in boiling water until tender. Retain a quarter of them and put the rest into a bowl with the olive oil, garlic and most of the lemon juice. Partly purée them in a food processor, then turn out into a bowl.

2 Add the mint, half the parsley, most of the Parmesan cheese and the mustard. Mix well. Put the mixture in the fridge to chill for about half an hour.

3 In the meantime, mix up the tomato, the remaining parsley, the olives, a squeeze of lemon juice, a splash of olive oil, the rest of the Parmesan and the retained whole broad beans.

4 To assemble the tartlets, simply spoon some of the puréed bean mixture into the tart cases and put some of the salad on top.

Floyd's onion tart, aka pissaladière

Most French bakers sell some sort of tart or quiche or slices of pizza. My favourite was, and is, the little individual onion tart known as a pissaladière. Sometimes it is prepared with bread dough cooked on a baking sheet and served in slices, and sometimes made as an individual tart in individual flan cases (about 10cm/4in across) with a buttery shortcrust pastry.

Total preparation/cooking time: 35 minutes plus chilling
Makes about 8 individual 10cm/4in tartlets

For the pastry
400g/14oz plain flour
a pinch of salt
200g/7oz butter
2–3 tbsp ice-cold water to bind

For the filling
a couple of pats of butter
2 large onions, cut in half and very, very finely sliced
1 egg yolk and 2 whole eggs, beaten together
about 240ml/8fl oz double cream or crème fraiche
salt and freshly ground black pepper

For the garnish
2 hard-boiled eggs, cut into 8 rings
8 slices of tomato
16 anchovy fillets in olive oil, drained
8 stoned black olives

1 To make the pastry, put the flour, salt and butter into a food processor and whiz round until the mixture resembles fine breadcrumbs. Gently trickle in enough water to bind the mixture into a soft ball. Wrap in cling film and leave in the refrigerator for at least half an hour before using. Or buy some ready-made shortcrust pastry.

2 Preheat the oven to 200°C/400°F/gas mark 6 and put a heavy baking sheet in the oven to heat up. To make the filling, melt the butter in a pan and sauté the onions until they are soft and translucent but not browned. Leave to cool while you roll out the pastry. Line the tart cases with the pastry and trim off the excess.

3 Beat the eggs and cream or crème fraîche together, season well with salt and pepper and stir in the onions. Pour this mixture into the uncooked pastry cases and cook in the oven for approximately 15 minutes. A quick peek after 15 minutes should reveal that the filling has risen a little like a soufflé and the pastry will have shrunk slightly from the sides of the tins. Remove from the oven and leave to cool on a wire rack. The filling will subside to level out. Whilst they are just warm, garnish each one with the slices of egg, tomato, anchovies and olive. Serve warm with a mixed green leaves salad and a mustard and garlic-based vinaigrette.

Oriental fish cakes with cucumber salad

You can make these fish cakes either in miniature 2.5cm/1in round patties and offer them as finger food at a drinks party, or you can make them much bigger and serve with a salad as a more substantial meal.

Total preparation/cooking time: 20 minutes
Makes about 10–12

450g/1lb skinned fillets of firm white fish, such as cod or
    haddock
2 eggs, beaten
1–2 tbsp red or green Thai curry paste
a good dash of fish sauce
a handful of chopped, mixed Kaffir lime leaves, basil
    leaves and coriander leaves
a little plain flour for dredging
groundnut or sunflower oil for deep-frying

1 Put the fish, eggs, curry paste and fish sauce in a food processor and whiz until smooth. Don't let the mixture become too runny.

2 Tip the mixture into a bowl and stir in the fresh herbs by hand. Still using your hands, form the mixture into small cakes about 5cm/2in wide. Dredge well with flour.

3 Heat 2.5 cm/1 inch oil in a wok and deep-fry the fish cakes for a few minutes until crisp and golden. Serve with the cucumber salad (see below).

Cucumber salad

Total preparation time: 5 minutes
Serves 4

2–3 shallots, grated
1 cucumber, peeled, deseeded and grated
2–3 red chillies, deseeded and chopped
2 tbsp dried prawn powder (available from Asian stores)
2 tbsp fish sauce
juice of ½ lemon or lime

1 Put all the ingredients into a bowl, mix well together and serve chilled.

Chilli chicken salad

Simple, zesty and refreshing, this makes the perfect brunch for the morning after the night before.

Total preparation/cooking time: 10 minutes
Serves 2

225g/8oz cooked chicken, minced
2 tbsp fish sauce
4 tbsp lime juice
2 spring onions, chopped
1 shallot, thinly sliced
2 tsp chopped fresh coriander
2 or 3 red or green fresh chillies, finely chopped
2 tbsp toasted, flaked almonds
a few fresh mint leaves

1 Mix together the chicken, fish sauce and lime juice. Then add the spring onions, shallot and coriander. Serve, sprinkled with fresh chillies, almonds and mint leaves.

Hot and sour duck salad

I include this recipe in memory of my friend Khun Akorn, who, with his chef Chom at the Tongsai Bay Hotel, Ko Samui, Thailand, taught me everything I know about Thai food and more.

Total preparation/cooking time: 20 minutes
Serves 4

4 duck breast fillets, roasted or grilled and thinly sliced
fresh crisp lettuce leaves
4 spring onions, finely chopped
2 shallots, thinly sliced
matchstick batons of celery and cucumber
chopped spring onions, celery leaves, sliced deseeded chilli, basil and mint leaves, to garnish

For the dressing
1 red and 1 green chilli, deseeded and very finely chopped
2 cloves garlic, crushed or finely chopped
1 teaspoon palm or demerara sugar
1–2 tbsp lime juice
3 tbsp fish sauce

1 Arrange the duck slices on a bed of lettuce on a serving dish. Sprinkle over the spring onions, shallots, celery and cucumber.

2 Put all the ingredients for the dressing into a small pan and heat through gently. The actual amount of ingredients is just a guide and you can experiment with it until it is to your liking. Pour the warm dressing over the salad and garnish with the chopped spring onions, celery leaves, sliced chilli, basil and mint.

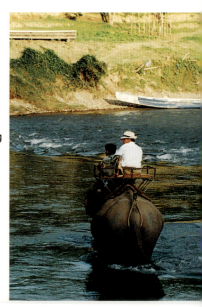

Hot and sour duck salad – soft and crunchy, simple and fresh

Monique Conil's tomato and cheese salad

Monique, the wife of my friend Pierre Conil, is and was a superb cook but she was so frustrated that her husband and I spent so much time in the Café de France (see Mediterranean omelette, page 36), she would only prepare food when she heard our car draw up. Consequently the spontaneity and freshness of her dishes was and is stunning. Take for example, this brilliant salad.

Total preparation/cooking time: 10 minutes
     plus chilling
Quantities are up to you, but let's say for 6 people

1kg/2¼lb tomatoes, some very ripe, some a little green,
     thinly sliced
175g/6oz mozzarella cheese, cut into 6mm/¼in cubes
fresh basil, chopped
1 tbsp caster sugar
1 wine glass olive oil
a couple of dashes white wine vinegar
sea salt and freshly ground black pepper

1 Put all the ingredients into a large salad bowl and mix gently. Refrigerate for at least 1 hour then toss gently again before serving.

And another brilliant dish she taught me was new potatoes and fresh herbs.

Simply boil some scrubbed, but not peeled, new potatoes in unsalted water until they are almost cooked, *al dente* you might say. Strain them carefully and put them, still hot, into a salad bowl. Leave them for 10 minutes so that they finish cooking in their own residual heat, then, while they are still warm, pour over a generous wine glass of the best quality olive oil. Then throw in a handful of chopped basil, mint and parsley leaves and chopped chives, mix well with a wooden spoon so that the potatoes are a little bit broken, and season with freshly ground black pepper and the superb salt, Fleur de sel de Camargue.

And by the way, this potato dish is a meal in its own right but can be served with, for example, grilled lamb chops.

Spanish broad bean salad

If the EU's food police decide to ban all vegetables, save two, I would go to the guillotine or confront the food police firing squad defiantly proclaiming the virtues of broad and butter beans. Herewith, a splendid salad.

Total preparation/cooking time: 15 minutes
Serves 4–6

1kg/2¼lb young broad beans (shelled weight)
200g/7oz thinly sliced serrano or better still Pate Negre, cut into very thin slivers
1 Cos lettuce, finely shredded
2 tbsp finely chopped fresh mint

For the dressing
2 cloves garlic, peeled
juice of 2 lemons
2 large tsp mild mustard
1 tsp sugar
olive oil
sea salt and freshly ground black pepper

1 Blanch the broad beans in a large pan of boiling salted water for 2–3 minutes. Drain and cool, then peel off and discard the thin skin from each bean. Mix the beans with the ham, lettuce and mint in a salad bowl.

2 To make the dressing, put the garlic, lemons, mustard and sugar into a blender and whiz, then gradually add enough olive oil to give a fairly thick emulsion. Season to taste, then pour the dressing over the salad and serve.

Another great way to eat cold, cooked and peeled broad beans is to fry them in a little olive oil with tiny cubes of Serrano ham, crushed garlic and parsley.

Tabbouleh

You will find this mouth-tingling dish all along the north African coast from Morocco right over to Egypt. It is street food and is normally prepared to order by the street hawkers and vendors. It's a dish that must be totally fresh, prepared instantly and must use the freshest of ingredients.

Total preparation/cooking time: 15 minutes
Serves 4–6

4 cups bulgar wheat
1 cup mixed finely chopped spring onions and red onion
1 cup skinned, deseeded and finely chopped tomatoes
2–3 cloves garlic, very finely crushed
1 cup each chopped fresh coriander and parsley
½ cup finely chopped fresh mint
at least 1 cup lemon juice
at least ½ cup good olive oil
sea salt and freshly ground black pepper

1 Prepare the bulgar wheat as instructed on the packet, then combine with all the remaining ingredients in a salad bowl and serve chilled.

Tunisian salad with pickled lemons

This Tunisian dish, known as Mechouia, is a salad of roasted or grilled peppers, onions and tomatoes, chopped up and mixed with lemon juice and olive oil. There are many variations of this salad but in my mind it is a cross between a ratatouille and a salad niçoise. It would be really authentic if you were to use the rind of pickled lemons (see below).

Total preparation/cooking time: 40 minutes
Serves 6

2 sweet onions
6 red and green peppers
4 large tomatoes
2 celery sticks, cut into 2.5cm/1in batons
1 tbsp chopped capers
2–3 chillies, deseeded and finely chopped
1 whole pickled lemon rind, finely diced (see below)
a handful of chopped fresh parsley
1 tsp ground coriander
lemon juice
olive oil
200g/7oz tuna in olive oil, drained and flaked
10 anchovy fillets in olive oil, drained
6 eggs, hard-boiled and cut into quarters

1 Preheat the oven to 220°C/425°F/gas mark 7. Roast the onions, peppers and tomatoes until blackened and tender (note that the onions will take longer than the peppers and tomatoes). Leave to cool, then remove the skin and, in the case of the peppers and tomatoes, the pith and seeds. Chop into pieces about 2.5cm/1in square.

2 Gently mix the tomatoes, peppers and onions together, then add the celery, capers, chillies, pickled lemon rind, parsley and ground coriander. Season to taste with lemon juice and olive oil. Tip onto a serving dish and arrange the flaked tuna, anchovy fillets and hard-boiled eggs on top.

Pickled lemons

And now for the pickled lemons, which, by the way, can be served chopped up with olives to eat with an aperitif, quartered and put onto lamb kebabs, or added to all kinds of salads and things like feta cheese. Anyway you need:

6 juicy lemons plus juice of 4 lemons
60g/2½oz coarse sea salt
240ml/8fl oz lemon juice
20ml/8fl oz lime juice (or juice of 6 or 7 limes)

1 Stand each lemon on its tail and, with a very sharp knife, cut a cross into the lemon so that it is in 4 quarters but still whole and connected at the bottom. Rub the insides of the lemons lavishly with the sea salt and reform them to their original shape.

2 Pack the lemons tightly into a sterilised Kilner jar then add the lime and lemon juice to cover the lemons completely. Seal the jar and keep in a cool place for about a month before using.

Salade niçoise

The composition of this splendid salad is open to interpretation and often it is interpreted badly. One thing is for sure, however, that a true Salade niçoise is not mixed with a French dressing of any sort and nor does it have garlic.

Total preparation/cooking time: 10 minutes
To serve 4 or 5 you need:

a selection of crisp and varied salad leaves, washed and thoroughly dried. You will also need some lightly cooked, cold French beans and some small, cold, boiled new potatoes, cut into thin slices, so cook and chill these first before you commence with the rest of the salad

8 ripe tomatoes, quartered and deseeded
2 green tomatoes, quartered and deseeded
½ tsp ground sea salt
5–6 tbsp olive oil
110g/4oz anchovy fillets in olive oil, drained
1 tin sardines in olive oil, drained
250g/9oz tuna fish in olive oil, drained
8 free-range eggs, hard-boiled and halved
150ml/5fl oz glistening black olives

1 Put the lettuce into a large salad bowl. Add the beans, potatoes, tomatoes, sea salt and olive oil and gently turn the salad until everything is coated with oil and salt.

2 Add all the other ingredients and, using your fingers, carefully mix them together, bringing the eggs and olives to the top.

Pok pok

Pok pok is roughly the Bangkok equivalent of a Latin-American guacamole, except instead of using avocado the Thais use papaya or mango. It is typical street food and is always served chilled.

Total preparation/cooking time: 10 minutes
    plus chilling
Serves 2–3

450g/1lb green papaya, grated, or mango, peeled and cut into cubes
1 tbsp roasted peanuts, chopped
1 tbsp dried shrimps
2–3 bird's-eye chillies, deseeded and chopped
3–4 cloves garlic, roughly chopped
1 tbsp brown sugar
a dash of fish sauce
fresh lime juice
2 tomatoes, skinned, deseeded and diced
110g/4oz cooked green beans, cut into 5cm/2in lengths

1 Put everything except the tomatoes and green beans into a food processor and whiz for a couple of seconds so that you have a lumpy purée. Pop onto a serving dish and chill. Then sprinkle over the tomatoes and beans and serve.

Spanish mountain breakfast - just the thing to get
you started in the morning

Spanish mountain breakfast

Sausage and beans, pork and beans and black pudding and beans are classical combinations – from the food of cowboys around the camp fire, to the great British banger and a tin of baked beans, through to the outstanding French cassoulet. I once spent a few days mountain biking and camping in the Sierra Nevada and on my trusty primus stove every day I prepared this breakfast or, if you like, brunch.

Total preparation/cooking time: 20 minutes
Enough for 2, or 1 large appetite

olive oil
2–3 cloves garlic, chopped
2 red peppers, cored, deseeded and sliced
2–3 chorizo sausage, sliced
2 morcilla (Spanish black sausage) or use about
    175g/6oz black pudding, sliced
175g/6oz canned haricot beans, drained
freshly ground black pepper

1 Heat the olive oil in a pan and throw in the garlic. Cook for a few moments then add the red peppers and sizzle together to get your tastebuds really going.

2 Add the sausages and cook for about 5-8 minutes. Stir in the beans and some black pepper and bubble them up, then cook gently until you can't wait any longer for breakfast – 5 minutes is time enough.

Spanish eggs

This makes a good starter or a wonderful light lunch. Because the peppers are already cooked, it's a quick and easy dish to do. It's good served with triangles of fried bread.

You will need 4 individual shallow ovenproof dishes.

Total preparation/cooking time: 20 minutes
Serves 4

300ml/½pt fresh tomato coulis or tomato sauce in one
    of those nice little cartons from the supermarket
4tbsp frozen petits pois
1 x 200g/7oz can red peppers, well drained and sliced
150g/5oz serrano ham, diced
½ tsp paprika
1 tbsp chopped fresh parsley
8 slices spicy sausage, ideally chorizo
8 eggs
salt and freshly ground black pepper

1 Preheat the oven to 200°C/400°F /gas mark 6. Divide the tomato sauce equally between 4 shallow ovenproof dishes. Pop some peas, peppers, ham, paprika, parsley and spicy sausage into each dish then crack two eggs into each dish over this mixture. Season with salt and pepper.

2 Cook in the oven for about 10 minutes, or until the egg whites are set but the yolks are still soft.

Deep-fried pancake (brik)

Brik is a crisp, deep-fried pancake made from semolina flour dough that is rolled out into very, very thin disks about 20.5cm/8in in diameter. You will be able to find brik pastry in good specialist shops and delicatessens. This Tunisian dish has relatives all over the world – the Vietnamese spring roll or the Chinese won ton or indeed the little parcels of filo pastry stuffed with cheese, spinach and other good things in Greece and Turkey. You can fill the pancake with just an egg or use other fillings (see below).

Total preparation/cooking time: 15 minutes
Serves 1

vegetable oil
1 brik pastry circle, 20cm/8in diameter, or use filo pastry
shredded crisp lettuce and lemon wedges, to serve

For the filling
1 egg or 1 egg and flaked tinned tuna fish, a few chopped capers, spring onions and parsley, or 1 egg and grated cheese, chopped ham, or 1 egg, cream cheese and chives

1 Heat the oil in a pan. Lay out the disc of pastry, place the filling into the centre and smear some of the egg white around the edges. Then fold it in half and squeeze the edges together for a half-moon shape.

2 Drop it into the hot oil for a few seconds until golden, then serve with lettuce and a lemon wedge.

Crostini

Crostini means 'little toasts' and in their simplest form are thin slices of bread, brushed with olive oil and toasted and then spread with a variety of savoury concoctions, or perhaps just rubbed with a raw clove of garlic and topped with a little chopped fresh tomato. Here and on the following pages are three of my special favourites.

Crostini with calves' liver

Total preparation/cooking time: 5 minutes
Serves 4–6

3 tbsp olive oil, plus extra, to serve
225g/8oz calves' liver, chopped into tiny cubes
1 clove garlic, finely chopped
1 very small onion, finely chopped
a good pinch of chopped fresh sage
salt and freshly ground black pepper
12 small slices of Italian country or French bread

1 Heat the olive oil in a small frying pan and add the calves' liver, garlic, onion and sage and fry briskly for a few seconds. Season to taste with salt and pepper.

2 Toast the bread, drizzle with oil, and top with the liver.

Crostini with calves' liver

Crostini - "little toasts"

Crostini with salt cod (see also Purée of salt cod, page 20)

Total preparation/cooking time: 20 minutes
    plus soaking
Serves 4–6

225g/8oz plump piece of salt cod, soaked overnight and
    drained
150ml/¼pt milk
1 clove garlic
4–6 tbsp olive oil
12 small slices of Italian country or French bread

1 Rinse the salt cod under fresh running water for about 20 minutes. Put it in a shallow pan with the milk and poach gently for about 20 minutes, until tender. Remove the skin and bones, then flake the fish into a bowl.

2 Purée the garlic in a mortar and pestle, then add the fish and pound it down until the fish is finely shredded. Using a jug, pour in the olive oil in a thin stream, pounding away at the same time to give a spreadable purée.

3 Toast the bread, drizzle with oil, and spread with the salt cod purée.

Crostini with roasted peppers

Total preparation/cooking time: 20 minutes
    plus marinating
Serves 4–6

2 red peppers
1 clove garlic, very finely chopped
3 tbsp olive oil
salt and freshly ground black pepper
12 small slices of Italian country or French bread

1 Preheat the oven to 220°C/425°F/gas mark 7. Put the peppers into a roasting tin and roast them until the skins blacken. When the peppers are cool, peel off the skins, cut in half and take out the pith and the pips. Chop the peppers finely.

2 Mix together the garlic and olive oil. Add the peppers and season well with salt and pepper. Leave to marinate for at least an hour.

3 Toast the bread, drizzle with the marinade, and top with the peppers.

Tomato and potato bhaji

On street stalls in India they cook this on a large round hotplate, and you can hear the click, click, click as they chop and scrape the sizzling ingredients into a smooth red purée rather like a tomato sauce. I suggest you use a very large, heavy frying pan.

Total preparation/cooking time: 50 minutes
Serves 6

vegetable oil
1tbsp mustard seeds
6 fresh curry leaves
4 fresh red chillies, finely chopped
1 large red onion, finely diced
ghee or unsalted butter
500g/1lb 2oz very ripe tomatoes, finely chopped
a pinch of ground turmeric
700g/1½lb cold mashed or chopped potato
a handful of chopped fresh coriander leaves
1tsp garam masala grains (available in supermarkets and delis, but if pushed use powdered garam masala)
salt
finely sliced red onion rings, lemon juice and ghee or unsalted butter, to serve

1 Heat a little oil in the pan and cook the mustard seeds until they crackle. Stir in the curry leaves, chillies and onion. Add some ghee or butter and cook until the onion is soft.

2 Stir in the tomatoes and turmeric. Season to taste with salt and cook gently, chopping all the time with a spoon or fork. When this mixture is becoming a purée, mix in the potato and continue chopping with your fork until the mixture is reduced to a thick purée. Stir in the chopped coriander and sprinkle on the garam masala.

3 Garnish with red onion rings and lemon juice. Just before serving, put a knob of ghee on each portion. Serve with thick slices of white bread.

Spicy herb oil

This oil is brilliant for adding flavour to all manner of dishes such as grills and barbecues, and is good shaken over pizzas.

Total preparation time: 5 minutes plus standing

4–5 sage leaves
4 red chillies
3 sprigs rosemary
4 sprigs thyme
6 bay leaves
30 black peppercorns
½ tsp fennel seeds
20 coriander seeds
best-quality vegetable oil (why not olive oil? I hear you cry. Well the spices and herbs cause the olive oil to break down)

1 Put all the herbs and spices into a 1 litre/1¾pt wine bottle, fill with the oil and seal with a cork. Leave for 2 weeks before using.

Kerala vegetable curry

Try to get as many interesting vegetables as you can for this spicy vegetable curry. Together with the fruit and coconut, they'll give it an authentic taste.

Total preparation/cooking time: 40 minutes
Serves 4

For the vegetables and fruit
You can use any vegetables you like, but they should
   all be cut into little batons of exactly the same size,
   for example potatoes, yam, green bananas, green
   beans, pumpkin, courgettes, peppers, mangoes.
   About 110g/4oz of each is about right.
3 dsp ground turmeric
salt

For the masala
6 or 8 very small red shallots, roughly chopped
5 or 6 fresh green chillies
2 cups grated fresh coconut (or you could used dried)
6 fresh curry leaves
1 tsp cumin seeds

For the garnish
coconut oil
a handful of small fresh curry leaves

1 To make the masala, grind all the ingredients to a paste, adding a little water if necessary.

2 Put all the vegetables and fruit into a large pan and just cover with water. Stir in the turmeric, season with salt, then bring to the boil and cook until the vegetables are almost cooked. Drain off and reserve the turmeric-flavoured water.

3 Stir the masala paste into the vegetables and add enough of the reserved turmeric-flavoured water to form a thick gravy. Continue cooking until the gravy has become creamy and spicy.

4 Just before serving, heat the coconut oil and quickly stir-fry the curry leaves and then sprinkle them over the vegetables.

An Indian vegetable mini-feast

The following four recipes should be cooked and served together with naan bread and chutneys. Each dish should be served in a small ramekin, or thali, as the Indians call it.

Spiced lentils

You can use black, yellow, green, whatever lentils you like, but the important thing is you must first wash them well and leave them to soak in fresh water for an hour.

Total preparation/cooking time: 1 hour
**   plus soaking**
Serves 4

200g/7oz dry lentils, well washed and soaked for 1 hour
1 tsp ground turmeric
vegetable oil
1 heaped tsp cumin seeds
2 red onions, finely chopped
1 tbsp mixed ginger and garlic purée (see page 76)
1 tbsp red chilli powder
3 tomatoes, finely chopped
salt

For the garnish
chopped fresh coriander leaves
4 fresh green chillies

1 Put the lentils, turmeric and some salt in a pan and pour in just enough water to cover. Cook until the lentils are tender but not completely cooked and the water has evaporated.

2 Heat the oil in a pan, add the cumin seeds and fry until they crackle. Then add the onions and sauté until golden brown. Stir in the ginger and garlic purée and the chilli powder. Stir-fry for 2-3 minutes, then add the tomatoes and cook for 15-20 minutes or until you have a coarse purée.

3 Add the parcooked lentils and simmer gently until they are tender. Serve garnished with the coriander leaves and a green chilli per person.

Onions stewed in yoghurt

Total preparation/cooking time: 20 minutes
Serves 4

120ml/4fl oz oil
1 tsp cumin seeds
1 heaped tbsp mixed ginger and garlic purée
   (see page 76)
500g/1lb 2oz baby onions of a uniform size

For the masala
about 50g/2oz natural yoghurt
2 tsp ground coriander
2 tsp ground turmeric
1 tsp red chilli powder
salt to taste

If you can't get baby onions, use medium-sized red onions, cut into quarters.

1 Mix together all the masala ingredients with ¼ cup of water.

2 Heat the oil in a pan, add the cumin seeds and fry until they crackle. Stir in the ginger and garlic purée and cook for a moment or two. Stir in the masala and then the onions, mixing thoroughly to ensure they are well coated with masala. Add about 1¼ cups of water and simmer gently over a low heat until the onions are tender but not losing their shape.

Indian cottage cheese in spinach purée

Unlike the European cottage cheese, paneer (Indian cottage cheese) is firm
and can be cut into cubes.

Total preparation/cooking time: 25 minutes
Serves 4

vegetable oil
400g/14oz paneer (Indian cottage cheese), cut into
   small cubes
800g/1¾lb spinach, well washed and drained
knob of butter or ghee
110g/4oz ghee
1 tsp cumin seeds
2 or 3 cloves garlic, peeled and finely chopped
1 tsp red chilli powder
2 tsp ground coriander
salt
120ml/4fl oz cream

1 Heat the vegetable oil in a large pan and fry the
paneer until golden on all sides, then remove from the
pan. Add a knob of butter or ghee to the pan and stir-
fry the spinach, then purée it in a blender.

2 Heat the ghee, add the cumin seeds and when
they crackle stir in the garlic and sauté until it is
golden brown. Add the spinach purée, chilli powder
and coriander. Season to taste with salt and cook for
3-4 minutes, stirring all the time.

3 Pop the paneer into the pan and simmer gently to
heat through. Stir in the cream and serve immediately.

Cumin potatoes

A very popular dish,
this works best with
firm potatoes that will
hold their shape when
cooked.

Total preparation/cooking time: 25 minutes
Serves 4

vegetable oil
1 heaped tsp cumin seeds
1 tbsp mixed ginger and garlic purée (see page 76)
1 tsp red chilli powder
500g/1lb 2oz parboiled potatoes, peeled and cut into
   2.5cm/1in cubes
salt

For the garnish
1 tsp garam masala
1 tsp ground coriander
chopped fresh coriander leaves

1 Heat some oil in a pan, add the cumin seeds and fry
until they crackle. Stir in the ginger and garlic purée
and sauté until slightly brown.

2 Add the chilli powder and enough water to make
a smooth, sauce-like gravy. Stir and season to taste
with salt.

3 Add the potatoes and mix them well into the gravy
then simmer gently until they are tender.

4 Garnish with the garam masala, ground coriander
and the chopped coriander leaves and serve.

New potatoes sautéed with mushrooms and onions

Serve this with chops or grilled chicken breast for a quick, but impressive, meal – although it's good enough to eat on its own.

Total preparation/cooking time: 30 minutes
Serves 4–6

approx 900g/2lb small, uniformly sized, scrubbed new potatoes, if possible ratte potatoes
olive oil or goose fat
butter
1 shallot, finely chopped
750g/1½lb wild mushrooms, e.g. chanterelles, girolles or morelles
1 sprig of thyme
225g/8oz baby onions, peeled
1 tbsp sugar
sea salt and freshly ground black pepper
chopped fresh chives, to garnish (optional)

1 Heat the olive oil or goose fat and sauté the potatoes gently until they are cooked and golden.

2 Meanwhile, heat some of the butter in a pan and sauté the shallot for a few minutes, then add the mushrooms, thyme and some sea salt and pepper. In another pan, just cover the onions with water and add a knob of butter and the sugar. Bring to the boil and then simmer gently for about 15 minutes or until the onions are almost cooked and the water has evaporated. Add a knob of butter and cook until the onions are lightly browned and glazed.

3 Mix the potatoes, mushrooms and onions in a serving dish, sprinkle with chives, if using, and serve.

Creamy spring or summer vegetables

Although this fragrant dish of vegetables can be served as an accompaniment, it is also a meal in itself.

Total preparation/cooking time: 35 minutes
Serves 4–6

about 600ml/1pt chicken or veal stock
8 baby carrots, scraped
3 large courgettes, halved, deseeded and quartered
225g/8oz white button mushrooms
225g/8oz wild mushrooms
4 baby turnips, peeled and cut in half
6–8 small spring onions, bulb only
150ml/¼pt double cream
50g/2oz unsalted butter
lemon juice
225g/8oz fresh spinach leaves, stalks removed, leaves roughly chopped
sea salt and freshly ground black pepper

1 Bring the stock to the boil in a pan and, starting with the carrots, cook each vegetable except the spinach separately in the stock, removing each one as it is done before adding the next lot. Put the cooked vegetables into a serving bowl and keep warm.

2 Boil the stock until reduced to about half to three-quarters of a cupful. Whisk in the cream, then whisk in little knobs of the butter until the sauce is thick. Season with lemon juice to taste. Add the spinach and heat through for 1 minute, then pour the sauce over the vegetables. Sprinkle on some sea salt and black pepper and serve.

New potatoes sautéed with mushrooms and onions –
an impressive, but quick, meal

Chilli and peanut vegetable salad – serve as an hors d'œuvre or as a snack

Chilli and peanut vegetable salad

This salad was one I encountered in Madagascar. It can be bought in the markets, where stallholders chop the ingredients with a mandoline, and it can be bought ready-made. Malagasy mustard seeds are tiny, rather like poppy seeds, so do not need to be crushed.

Total preparation/cooking time: 15 minutes
Serves 6–8

3 onions, halved and finely sliced
6 carrots, grated
½ white cabbage, shredded
110g/4oz French or runner beans, sliced
handful of fresh peanuts, crushed
salt

For the dressing
3 garlic cloves, crushed
2 very small red chillies, chopped
25g/1oz fresh root ginger, chopped
1 tsp mustard seeds, crushed
1 tsp curry powder
½ tsp ground turmeric
40ml/1½fl oz white wine vinegar
120ml/4fl oz groundnut oil

1 To make the dressing, mix all the ingredients together.

2 Toss the vegetables in the dressing, sprinkle with the peanuts and season with salt to taste.

Sweet and sour aubergines

I learnt this stunning dish of creamy baby aubergines cooked in an exotic tomato and onion gravy from the charming head chef of the Fisherman's Cove Hotel, near Madras. He stressed the importance of obtaining aubergines that are all roughly the size of a duck egg.

Total preparation/cooking time: 50 minutes
Serves 4

500g/1lb 2oz baby aubergines, stalks removed and cut in half lengthways (if you can't get baby aubergines, make sure you cut the aubergines into identical size chunks with the skin on)
vegetable or coconut oil
3 red onions, finely sliced
4 tomatoes, coarsely chopped
15–20 fresh curry leaves
200g/7oz grated fresh coconut
2 tsp ground turmeric
2 tbsp chilli powder
2 tbsp ground coriander
200g/7oz tamarind purée, available from Asian stores
salt
chopped fresh coriander leaves, to garnish

1 Heat some oil in a pan and sauté the onions until they are completely soft. Add the tomatoes and cook until you have a thick, rich onion and tomato gravy. If necessary, add a little water, but be sure to cook until the water evaporates, leaving a thick, red gravy. Stir in the curry leaves.

2 Meanwhile, heat some oil in a pan and shallow-fry the aubergines until they are half-cooked, then put to one side.

3 Whiz the coconut to a paste in a food processor, adding a little water if necessary, or use canned, creamed coconut. Mix together the powdered spices, tamarind and coconut paste and stir into the thickened tomato and onion gravy. Season with salt.

4 Cook for a couple of minutes, mixing well, then add the aubergines and simmer gently for about 20 minutes until the aubergines are fully cooked. Garnish with the coriander leaves and serve.

Chilled courgettes in lemon sauce

An unusual way to serve courgettes, especially in the summer when they are at their best.

Total preparation/cooking time: 30 minutes plus chilling
Serves 4

4–5 courgettes, sliced into batons about 2.5cm/1in long
oil for frying
a pinch of cumin seeds
3 juicy lemons, peeled, cut into segments and all pith removed
1 medium onion, very finely sliced
about 150ml/¼pt chicken stock
1 heaped tbsp white sugar
1 tbsp grated fresh root ginger
a dash of sesame, hazelnut or walnut oil
chopped fresh parsley or coriander
pickled lemon zest, see page 44 (optional)
salt and freshly ground black pepper

1 Heat some oil in a shallow pan, add the cumin seeds and cook until they crackle, just a few seconds. Add the courgettes and onion and fry very quickly just to brown them a little bit. Add the chicken stock, lemons, sugar and ginger and simmer gently for 15-20 minutes until the courgettes are cooked. Season with salt and pepper, then chill before serving.

2 To serve, garnish with chopped fresh parsley or coriander and if you have any pickled lemons dice some of the lemon peel very finely and sprinkle over the dish.

Sautéed mushrooms with tomato

This is a great dish to serve on crispy slices of fried bread.

Total preparation/cooking time: 30 minutes
Serves 4–6

750g/1¾lb mixed wild mushrooms, wiped and roughly
   chopped
5 tbsp olive oil
1 onion, finely chopped
2–3 large tomatoes, skinned, deseeded and chopped
2 bay leaves
1 sprig rosemary
salt and freshly ground black pepper

1 Heat the olive oil in a large frying pan. Add the
onion and sauté until transparent, about 3-4 minutes.
Stir in the tomato, bay leaves and the rosemary.

2 Cook for a couple of minutes, then add the
mushrooms and continue to cook over a low heat for
about 20 minutes, stirring every now and again.
Season with some salt and pepper, take out the bay
leaves, and serve.

Sautéed mushrooms with
tomato - terrific on its own
or on fried bread

Ratatouille

This classic Provençale dish should not be overcooked so that it resembles a mush of vegetables in tomato sauce, but it must be cooked gently and simply so that each vegetable retains its individual flavour.

**Total preparation/cooking time: 45 minutes
    plus chilling**
Serves 4–6

1 aubergine
1 courgette
1 red pepper
1 green pepper
2 onions
10 tomatoes, cut into quarters and deseeded
best-quality olive oil
10 cloves garlic, coarsely chopped
parsley, finely chopped
salt and freshly ground black pepper
sprig of fresh thyme

1 The vitally important thing about ratatouille is that each vegetable is cooked separately. So cut all the vegetables into equal-sized pieces – fork-sized, perhaps. Prepare the aubergine and courgette first. Sprinkle them with salt and leave them to 'sweat'. Then dry with kitchen paper.

2 Heat some olive oil in a large frying pan and cook each vegetable, seasoned with salt and pepper, one after the other, until they are tender, then put to one side with all the juices from the pan. During this process, if necessary, top up the oil from time to time.

3 Now put the lot into a saucepan, add the garlic, parsley and thyme and all the left-over oil and cook for 10-15 minutes to amalgamate the flavours. Leave to cool, refrigerate and eat cold.

A gratin of Swiss chard

Chard is a member of the beet family; look out for firm, crisp stalks and avoid any that are flabby and soft.

Total preparation/cooking time: 30 minutes
Serves 4–6

1kg/2¼lb Swiss chard, stalks cut into 2.5cm/1in batons, greens finely shredded
50g/2oz butter
2 tbsp flour
600ml/1pt milk, warmed
75g/3oz Gruyère cheese, grated
mature Parmesan cheese, grated
salt and freshly ground black pepper

1 First, blanch the chard stalks in boiling salted water until tender but not overcooked, strain and put to one side. Stir-fry the shredded greens in a little butter until they too are tender but still slightly undercooked and put to one side.

2 Meanwhile, melt the butter in a pan, add the flour and stir until you have a smooth roux. Slowly add the milk and stir until you have a smooth, thick, white sauce. Over a low heat stir in the grated Gruyère cheese and season with salt and pepper.

3 Preheat the grill. Put the drained chard stalks and greens into a gratin dish, cover with the sauce and sprinkle liberally with the Parmesan cheese. Pop under the grill until golden and bubbling.

Green tomatoes Bombay-style

Serve this dish with some rice and deep-fried crispy Bombay duck, which are, in fact, sun-dried small fish available from Asian stores.

Total preparation/cooking time: 15 minutes
Serves 4

500g/1lb 2oz firm, green tomatoes, cut into quarters and deseeded
vegetable oil
½ tsp fenugreek seeds
½ tsp cumin seeds
2 or 3 fresh green chillies, coarsely chopped
salt

For the masala
1 heaped tsp garlic purée (see page 76)
1 tsp red chilli powder
½ tsp ground turmeric
2 tsp ground coriander
1 tsp sugar

1 To make the masala, mix together all the ingredients with a little water to form a very dry paste.

2 Heat the oil in a pan and fry the fenugreek and cumin seeds until they crackle. Stir in the masala and cook for 2–3 minutes, then add the chillies and tomatoes and season to taste with salt. Mix well and cook gently until the tomatoes start to soften.

Spiced beetroot

When in Scandinavia I eat pickled beetroot and herrings for breakfast. When I was a kid, my favourite sandwich on my fishing trips was slices of my mum's home-made beetroot pickle in malt vinegar between thick slices of bread and butter. Crispy, deep-fried chips of beetroot can go well with fish, little young beetroots can be roasted with pheasant and guinea fowl, but the best beetroot dish I have ever had was in Madras.

Total preparation/cooking time: 40 minutes
Serves 4–6

800g/1¾lb fresh beetroot, boiled, skinned and chopped
   into small cubes
120ml/4fl oz coconut oil
1 heaped tbsp black mustard seeds
150g/5oz red shallots, finely chopped
6 or 8 fresh green chillies, finely
150g/5oz grated fresh coconut
salt and freshly ground black pepper

1 Heat the coconut oil, add the mustard seeds and fry until they crackle. Stir in the shallots and chillies and sauté for 2-3 minutes.

2 Add the grated coconut and stir-fry until it is slightly brown and toasted. Stir in the beetroot and mix well with the other ingredients. Season with salt and pepper and serve.

Walnut sauce

Great served with ribbon pasta, as they do in Italy, this rich sauce also
goes well with grilled chicken or white fish, or with roasted vegetables.

Total preparation/cooking time: 5 minutes
Serves 4

50g/2oz shelled walnuts
25g/1oz butter
1 tbsp extra-virgin olive oil
225ml/8fl oz double cream
salt and freshly ground black pepper

1 Whiz the walnuts in a food processor or blender until fairly fine but not powdered – the sauce is best a little crunchy.

2 Melt the butter and olive oil in a saucepan. Stir in the ground nuts, then add the cream and season to taste with salt and pepper. Bring just to the boil, then lower the heat and simmer for about 2 minutes, until thickened.

Plum tomato sauce

Only make this if you have the sweetest, ripest tomatoes. Alternatively,
go and buy one of those super tomato sauces that come in a box from
the supermarket.

Total preparation/cooking time: 30 minutes
Makes about 300ml/½pt

1kg/2¼lb very ripe plum tomatoes, skinned, deseeded
    and chopped
4 tbsp extra-virgin olive oil
1 onion, finely chopped
1 large clove garlic, crushed
1 tsp caster sugar
1 tbsp chopped fresh basil
wine vinegar
salt and freshly ground black pepper

1 Heat the olive oil in a large, heavy-based saucepan. Add the onion and fry for about 3–4 minutes until it is transparent, then add the tomatoes, garlic, caster sugar, basil and a few drops of wine vinegar. Season with salt and pepper then simmer slowly for as long as it takes to get a rich, thick, red sauce.

Three methods of cooking rice

It is important to buy the best quality rice you can, and for each of the following three recipes make sure you rinse the rice thoroughly under cold running water for at least 15 minutes to eliminate the excess starch, then strain well so that no water at all is left.

Lemon-flavoured rice

Total preparation/cooking time: 30 minutes
Serves 4

1½ cups long-grain rice, washed thoroughly
ghee
vegetable oil
1 tsp black mustard seeds
1 green chilli, finely chopped
3 or 4 dried red chillies, coarsely chopped
½ tsp finely chopped root ginger
small handful fresh curry leaves
1 heaped tbsp unsalted cashew nuts
½ tsp ground turmeric
juice of 2 lemons
salt
chopped fresh coriander leaves, to garnish

1 Put the rice in a pan with plenty of salted water, bring to the boil and then give it one quick stir. Continue cooking until the rice is just tender. Drain thoroughly, transfer to a bowl and stir in a heaped tbsp of ghee. Set aside.

2 Heat some oil in a large shallow frying pan, add the mustard seeds and cook until they crackle. Add the chillies, ginger, curry leaves and cashew nuts and quickly stir-fry. Sprinkle in the turmeric, stir in the lemon juice, a pinch of salt and about ¼ cup of water. Simmer the mixture for 2–3 minutes until you have a turmeric-coloured gravy.

3 Add the rice to the gravy, stir to combine and continue cooking until the liquid has been absorbed and the rice is completely tender. Serve sprinkled with chopped coriander leaves.

Cumin rice

**Total preparation/cooking time: 30 minutes
    plus soaking**
Serves 6

500g/1lb 2oz basmati rice, washed under running water
    for at least 15 minutes, then strained
50ml/2fl oz vegetable oil
1 tsp black peppercorns
1 heaped tbsp cumin seeds
1 bay leaf
4 green cardamom pods
5 broken pieces of cinnamon stick
1 heaped tbsp of ghee or butter
salt
chopped fresh mint, basil and coriander leaves, to
    garnish

1 Soak the washed rice in fresh water for 30 minutes,
then drain thoroughly.

2 Heat the oil in a shallow frying pan, add the
peppercorns, cumin seeds and bay leaf and cook until
they crackle.

3 Add the rice, cardamom and cinnamon and stir-fry
in the oil for 10 minutes, stirring continuously. Add
1 litre/1¾pts boiling water, season with salt, cover and
cook for 8 minutes. Stir the rice once, add the ghee or
butter then replace the lid and cook for a further 7
minutes, or until the water has evaporated and the
rice is tender. Serve sprinkled with chopped fresh
herbs.

Coconut rice

Don't use rice that is old or too dry as it will need
more water to cook in.

Total preparation/cooking time: 30 minutes
Serves 8

450g/1lb long-grain rice, washed thoroughly and
    drained
750ml/1¼pts thin coconut milk
1 tsp salt

1 Put the rice in a heavy pan, add the coconut milk
and salt and bring to the boil, stirring. Reduce the
heat, cover with a tight-fitting lid, and simmer gently
for 12 minutes.

2 Take the pan off the heat and leave with the lid on
for a further 10 minutes. It will finish cooking in its own
steam. Fluff up with a fork before serving or, much
better still, buy something like an electric rice cooker
because this will cook your rice perfectly and keep it
warm until you want to eat it.

Substantial Lunch and Supper Dishes

I really, really enjoy a roast leg of lamb with onion sauce or a really succulent, fatty, rare rib of roast beef with golden roast potatoes. But these dishes and others like them are not exactly exciting to cook, so I have cultivated a group of friends who I know can prepare these dishes to perfection, and when I hunger for such a meal, I contrive to get myself invited to lunch (that includes you, Alistair and Jan!). They know who they are, dear reader, and I am certainly not giving their addresses out. So the sorts of dishes I like to cook at home tend to involve quite a lot of movement, quick chopping, quick stirring with lots of colour and not too much involvement and certainly no serious weighing and measuring quantities and it seems to me, if there are two of you and you are cooking for example Thai green chicken curry (see page 82) you don't need to be a rocket scientist to work out how many bits and pieces you need to chuck into your wok. So, what I am trying to say here is, please approach these recipes with an open mind and apply some common sense. Timings and measurements are all absolutely approximate.

So, please turn up the gas, pour yourself a large one and enjoy your cooking as much as your eating. Bon appetit!

Please note: Most of the recipes in this section are jolly quick and easy to prepare, with the exception of some of my absolute favourites that will require a little more time and effort – but they'll be worth it.

Floyd's couscous

Although this dish has lots of ingredients and takes a bit longer than most of the recipes in the book, it is actually very simple to prepare. It is also a very versatile dish because you can have a meat couscous, chicken couscous, vegetable couscous etc., etc. In former times, cooking the couscous grains was quite a chore, but these days you can buy quick-cook couscous very easily.

Total preparation/cooking time: 1¼ hours
Serves 10

500g/1lb 2oz young carrots, scraped
500g/1lb 2oz young turnips, peeled
500g/1lb 2oz young courgettes, trimmed
oil
500g/1¼lb stewing lamb or mutton, cut into cubes
2 cans chickpeas, drained and rinsed
4 large onions, coarsely chopped
6 tomatoes, coarsely chopped
300g/11oz raisins
3–4 chillies, chopped
1 heaped tsp harissa paste (a purée of chillies, garlic, coriander and salt, available in tins)
1 tbsp ground coriander
a large pinch of saffron
500g/1¼lb free-range chicken, cut into pieces on the bone
500g/1¼lb little red spicy beef or pork sausages known as Merguez
2 boxes ready-cooked couscous
a large knob of butter
chopped fresh herbs, such as chives and coriander (optional)
sea salt and freshly ground black pepper
extra coriander and harissa, to serve

1 Cut the carrots and turnips to the size of the courgettes.

2 Heat the oil in a large pan and quickly brown the lamb. Add the chickpeas, onions, tomatoes, raisins, chillies, harissa, coriander and saffron. Barely cover with water, bring to the boil and simmer for about 30 minutes. Then add the chicken pieces and cook for another 15 minutes, then add the carrots and, 10 minutes later, the turnips and the sausages, and then a few minutes later the courgettes. Season with salt and pepper. The reason for this is that the meats and the vegetables will all cook at different speeds and you must stagger them so that they all arrive perfectly cooked.

3 Prepare the couscous according to the instructions on the packet, stir in the butter and fork through some of the chopped herbs, if using. Make a mound of the couscous in a warm serving dish and cover with the vegetables and meat, a little of the cooking liquid and garnish with fresh coriander. Serve the rest of the cooking liquid, or bouillon as it should be called, separately with a dish of harissa for those who would like theirs a little spicier.

Marrakesh lamb tagine with prunes

This is another classic dish from Morocco and, like the couscous, comes in many different styles and flavours. Classically they are cooked very slowly over charcoal in an earthenware dish with a funnel-shaped lid. This, again, takes a bit longer than most of the recipes in the book but the flavours are superb and well worth the wait.

Total preparation/cooking time: 1½ hours
Serves 6–8

1 shoulder of lamb, boned and cut into bite-sized pieces
butter
2 onions, finely diced
2–4 cloves garlic, finely chopped
1 tbsp tomato purée
1½ tsp ground ginger
a large pinch of saffron strands
1½ tsp ground coriander
1 cinnamon stick
4 tomatoes, finely chopped
20 small shallots or silver-skinned onions, peeled
250g/9oz stoned, ready-to-eat prunes
250g/9oz dried apricots
1 tsp honey
½ cup sliced almonds, toasted
sea salt and freshly ground black pepper
chopped fresh coriander leaves, to garnish

1 Heat some butter in a large pan, add the meat and fry until browned on all sides. Add the onions and garlic and cook until golden. Next, stir in the tomato purée, ginger, saffron, coriander and cinnamon stick. Season with salt and pepper and add the chopped tomatoes. Cook over a low heat for 5–10 minutes and then pour in enough water to cover. As this dish is not meant to be swimming in sauce, you must not add too much liquid. If it gets too dry during the cooking process you can add small amounts of water as you go along. Add the bone from the shoulder of lamb and simmer gently for 30 minutes.

2 Meanwhile, fry the shallots in butter until golden. Add them to the lamb and continue cooking until the lamb is tender, probably another hour. It should be a thick, rich, spicy stew. Stir in the prunes, apricots and honey, transfer to a serving dish and sprinkle over the toasted almonds. Garnish with the coriander leaves and serve.

Rasheed mutton curry

The cooking in Kerala, South India is spicy and creamy and, in my view, some of the best food in India comes from this region. There are vast coconut plantations, so coconut milk and coconut flesh are liberally employed in the preparation of many dishes. While I was staying in the charming Malabar Hotel in Cochin, I spent a lot of time in the kitchen with my now friend, Rasheed, the head chef. This is one of many dishes he taught me to make.

Total preparation/cooking time: 1 hour
plus marinating
Serves 4–6

1kg/2¼lb mutton or lamb, cut into bite-sized morsels
2 x 400ml/14fl oz cans coconut milk
coconut oil
150g/5oz small red shallots, coarsely chopped
1 tsp small black mustard seeds
4 or 5 fresh green chillies, chopped
1 dsp puréed fresh garlic
1 dsp puréed root ginger
1 sprig of fresh curry leaves
200g/7oz peeled potatoes, cut into bite-sized pieces
2 dsp whole garam masala (this will be about 6 or 7
    cardamom pods, ½ cinnamon stick, 6 or 7 cloves,
    and 2 or 3 bay leaves)
salt
chopped fresh coriander leaves, to garnish

For the masala
2 tsp chilli powder
1 tsp ground cumin
2 tsp ground coriander

1 Mix half a can of coconut milk with twice that quantity of water to thin it. Marinate the cubed mutton or lamb in the milk for about 2 hours in the fridge. To make the masala, mix all the ingredients and set aside.

2 Heat some coconut oil in a large pan and fry the shallots until golden. Add the mustard seeds and fry until they crackle, then add the chillies. Stir in the puréed garlic and ginger and the curry leaves, then mix in the masala and sauté until you have a rich paste.

3 Add the mutton or lamb with its marinade to the pan and push down so that it is completely covered by the other ingredients. Add the whole garam masala. Bring to the boil and simmer for about 20 minutes, then add the potato chunks and season with salt. From time to time, as the liquid in the pan reduces, gradually add the remaining coconut milk until you have a thick, rich gravy and the meat and potatoes are tender. Serve garnished with coriander leaves.

Rogan josh

Rogan josh is a slow-simmered dish that results in a smooth, rich and spicy gravy enriched with ground almonds. You can use chicken, beef or lamb although, by the way, while lamb features on the menus in India, they invariably use goat, and very good it is, too.

To make the ginger and garlic purée, just combine equal quantities of peeled ginger and garlic, and purée in a food processor. To make the brown onion paste, finely dice some red onions and sauté them in ghee or oil until golden brown, then purée in a food processor.

Total preparation/cooking time: 1 hour
Serves 4

800g/1¾lb lamb, mutton, beef or chicken, cut into bite-
    sized morsels (if using chicken, cut it into chunks,
    but leave it on the bone, this enriches the sauce)
1 cup yoghurt
½ cup tomato purée
1 tbsp ground almonds
salt

For the masala
vegetable oil, for frying
3 or 4 cloves
4 or 5 whole cardamon pods
4 tbsp ginger and garlic purée (see above)
2 tbsp brown onion paste (see above)
½ tbsp garam masala
1 tsp chilli powder

For the garnish
chopped fresh coriander leaves
2.5cm/1in piece of root ginger, peeled and cut into very
    thin sticks
a generous pinch of saffron threads soaked in 3 tbsp
    rosewater

1 To make the masala, heat some oil in a large pan, add the cloves and cardamom pods and fry until they crackle. Add the rest of the masala ingredients and stir-fry for a minute or two.

2 Add the lamb and yoghurt to the pan, season with salt and cook for 3-4 minutes so that the meat is well covered with the masala and yoghurt. Add a little water and simmer gently until the lamb is almost tender.

3 Stir the tomato purée into the pan and continue cooking, uncovered, until you have reduced the liquid by about one third. Stir in the ground almonds.

4 Garnish with chopped coriander leaves and the ginger julienne, sprinkle the saffron and rosewater over the top and serve with rice, poppadoms, chutney, yoghurt, etc., etc.

Garlic-roasted chicken

A feast for garlic-lovers, this dish can be popped in the oven
while you go off and do whatever it is you have to do. A salad
goes very nicely with this chicken.

Total preparation/cooking time: 1½ hours
Serves 4

1 corn-fed chicken
juice of 1 lemon
50g/2oz butter
1kg/2¼lb plump cloves garlic, half in their skin, half
    peeled
1 bay leaf
1 sprig thyme
olive oil
1 glass dry white wine
salt and freshly ground black pepper

1 Preheat the oven to 200°C/400°F/gas mark 6.
Rub the chicken inside and out with salt, pepper and
25g/1oz of the butter, and squeeze lemon juice inside
and over the skin. Stuff the bird with 450g/1lb of the
peeled garlic, the bay leaf and the thyme.

2 Heat some olive oil in a large frying pan and brown
the chicken all over, then transfer it to a roasting tin,
breast down. Cook in the oven for about 30 minutes,
or until the chicken has started to brown. Add the
remaining unpeeled garlic and 1-2 tbsp olive oil to the
tin, turn the chicken onto its back, baste and continue
roasting for approximately 1 hour. (Remember that it
will take a little longer than usual because of the
stuffing.)

3 When the chicken is cooked, remove it and the
roasted unpeeled garlic onto a warm serving dish. Add
a glass of dry white wine to the juices in the roasting
tin, bubble for a moment or two, whisk in a large knob
of butter, then season with salt and pepper and strain
over the chicken.

Sauté of chicken à la crème - at its most superb when
made with a free-range, corn-fed chicken

Sauté of chicken à la crème

This delicate and delicious recipe is a dish typical of the better quality restaurants in the Loire valley. To make it really superb you must use at least free-range, corn-fed chicken or, even better still, a *poulet de Bresse.*

Total preparation/cooking time: 1 hour
Serves 4

1 free-range, corn-fed chicken, approximately
    1.75kg/4lb, cut into 8 pieces
200g/7oz unsalted butter
12 small shallots, peeled
juice of 1 lemon
about 500ml/18fl oz Pouilly-Fumé or other dry Loire
    white wine
250g/9oz chanterelles, morels or ceps, chopped
300ml/½pt double cream
1 tbsp chopped fresh tarragon leaves
1 egg yolk
salt and freshly ground black pepper

1 Heat some of the butter in a large sauté pan and fry the chicken and the shallots until the shallots are golden brown, then turn down the heat, add the lemon juice, and sauté gently for 20 minutes.

2 Add enough wine to just cover the chicken and bring to the boil. Reduce the heat, cover and simmer gently for about 15 minutes, until the chicken is almost done. Meanwhile, fry the mushrooms in the remaining butter, add to the chicken and simmer for a further 10 minutes. Remove the chicken, mushrooms and shallots to a serving dish and keep warm.

3 Reduce the wine and juices by half over a high heat and season with salt and pepper. Reduce the heat and gently whisk in the cream and the tarragon. Take the sauce off the heat and whisk in, very quickly, the egg yolk. Pour the thickened sauce over the chicken and vegetables (do not attempt to reheat it, or the sauce will curdle) and serve immediately.

Alsace chicken

Actually, this Alsacienne dish is best made with very strong lager. Serve it with some fresh pasta.

Total preparation/cooking time: 1¼ hours
Serves 6

1 x 1.5kg/4lb corn-fed chicken, quartered
225g/8oz butter
oil
4 shallots, finely chopped
200g/7oz mushrooms, sliced
1 small glass Marc d'Alsace or gin
350ml/12fl oz strong lager or pale ale
a dash of Guinness
300ml/½pt double cream
salt and freshly ground black pepper
finely chopped fresh parsley, to garnish

1 Melt 200g/7oz of the butter and a little oil in a pan and sauté the chicken pieces until lightly browned. Add the shallots and mushrooms and cook until well browned. Then flame with the Marc d'Alsace or gin and, when the flames have died down, pour in the lager. Season with salt and pepper and simmer on a gentle heat for about 1 hour, or until the chicken is tender.

2 Arrange the chicken pieces in a deep serving dish and keep hot. On a high heat, reduce the sauce by half, add a dash of Guinness then whisk in the cream and, finally, the remaining butter, just to thicken the sauce. Pour the sauce over the chicken, sprinkle with the parsley and serve.

Creamy chicken curry

This super dish is delicate but outrageously rich. If you are allergic to dairy products or nuts or are at all health conscious, don't cook it!

Total preparation/cooking time: 45 minutes
    plus marinating
Serves 4

1kg/2¼lb boneless chicken morsels
lemon juice
ghee or butter
4 or 5 green cardamom pods, crushed
7.5cm/3in cinnamon stick broken into flakes
3 or 4 whole cloves
3 or 4 cloves garlic, peeled and puréed
4cm/1½inch piece fresh root ginger, peeled and puréed
225g/8oz red onions, boiled, drained and puréed
1 cup natural yoghurt
a very generous pinch of saffron threads soaked in a
    dash of rosewater
110g/4oz unsalted cashew nuts soaked in a little milk
    for 1 hour and then puréed
½ cup double cream
salt
chopped fresh coriander leaves and silver leaf (available
    from good Asian stores), to garnish

1 Put the chicken in a bowl, sprinkle with salt and lemon juice and leave to marinate for 1 hour.

2 Heat some ghee or butter in a large pan and sauté the cardamom pods, cinnamon and cloves for 1-2 minutes, then add the puréed garlic, ginger and onions and stir-fry until the mixture turns golden. Reduce the heat and stir in the yoghurt and the saffron.

3 Add the chicken pieces and simmer gently for 5-10 minutes, then stir in the cashew nut purée and mix well. Continue cooking gently until the chicken is tender, then stir in the double cream and cook for a few more minutes. Garnish with chopped coriander leaves and silver leaf and serve.

Tandoori chicken with apple and mint chutney

The reason that Tandoori chicken is so delicious in India is that they use those scrawny tough old birds with very long legs that are pecking about all over the place. Also, it is always served on the bone, which gives the chicken its additional flavour, and, unlike in certain restaurants I could name, the tandoori marinade is not dyed with food colouring. I have assumed that you don't have a tandoori oven so I have adapted the recipe for domestic ovens. If you do happen to have a tandoori oven you are so smart you don't need this recipe!

**Total preparation/cooking time: 50 minutes
    plus marinating
Serves 4–6**

1 chicken, skinned, cut in half lengthways and scored
    on breast, thighs and legs
vegetable oil for basting

For the chilli marinade
2 tsp red chilli powder
a large pinch of salt
lemon juice

For the creamy marinade
1 tsp garlic purée (see page 76)
1 tsp ginger purée (see page 76)
1 tsp ground cumin
a pinch of saffron threads
about 1 cup cream
about 1 cup yoghurt

For the chutney
cubes of peeled apple
a handful of fresh mint leaves
a handful of fresh coriander leaves

For the garnish
some very crisp lettuce leaves
some very thin slices of red onion
wedges of lemon or lime

1 To make the chilli marinade, mix the chilli powder and salt with enough lemon juice to make a paste to rub all over the chicken. Smear it over the chicken and leave for 30 minutes. Meanwhile, make the chutney by whizzing the apple, mint and coriander quickly in a food processor, then chill in the fridge until required.

2 Whisk all the ingredients for the creamy marinade into a thick paste and liberally smear over the chicken. Put in the fridge to marinate for at least 3 hours.

3 Preheat the oven to 120°C/250°F/gas mark ½. Place the chicken on a roasting rack with the tray underneath to catch any drips and bake in the oven for about 20 minutes, then turn up the heat to at least 180°/350°F/gas mark 4 and cook until the chicken is almost ready. (Or you can of course cook this on a barbeque.) Baste with oil and cook for a further couple of minutes, if necessary – the chicken should be slightly crispy or even a little bit burnt on the outside but moist and tender on the inside.

4 Garnish with lettuce, onion and lemon or lime wedges, and serve with the chutney.

Thai green chicken curry

This is excellent served with steamed rice and a glass of
freshly squeezed lime juice.

Total preparation/cooking time: 15 minutes
Serves 4

450g/1lb boned free-range chicken, sliced thinly
3 tbsp coconut or corn oil
3 tbsp Thai green curry paste
60ml/2fl oz coconut milk or dilute some of the coconut
    cream with water
3 tbsp fish sauce
3 tbsp deseeded and sliced mixed red and green chillies
3 tbsp brown sugar
1 cup frozen petits pois
1 tbsp fresh or tinned green peppercorns
2 fistfuls of fresh basil leaves
3 tbsp coconut cream

1 Heat the oil in a wok or large frying pan. Stir in the curry paste then add the chicken and stir-fry quickly over a high heat, stirring and tossing it in the oil and paste, for 2–3 minutes.

2 Add the coconut milk, fish sauce, chillies and sugar. Cook for 5 minutes, stirring well. Just before serving, stir in the peas and peppercorns – the peas need to be hot, not cooked. Finally, toss in the basil leaves and add a spoonful of coconut cream on top of each serving.

Saigon-style chicken with lemon grass

Another dish I
discovered on my
travels in Vietnam. Be
very careful not to burn
the sugar.

Total preparation/cooking time: 30 minutes
    plus marinating
Serves 4

900g/2lb free-range chicken breast fillets, skinned and
    cubed
2 tsp finely chopped garlic
1 blade of lemon grass, finely chopped
2 tbsp fish sauce
3 tbsp white sugar
1 tsp freshly ground black pepper
2 tbsp groundnut oil
slivers of deseeded red chilli
fresh coriander and basil leaves

1 Mix together the garlic, lemon grass, fish sauce, 1 tbsp of the sugar and the pepper and marinate the chicken in the mixture for 30 minutes.

2 Heat the oil in a large frying pan or wok, add the chicken and its marinade to the pan and sauté until golden and tender, stirring all the time.

3 Meanwhile, put the remaining sugar in a very small pan over a medium heat and caramelise. Don't take your eyes off it as it turns liquid and bubbly. As soon as it becomes golden brown, take it off the heat. Immediately stir in the slivers of chilli and mix them into the chicken. Heat through, garnish with coriander and basil leaves and serve with steamed rice.

Thai green chicken curry
- a simple Thai dish

Chicken laksa

You will find versions of this Malaysian coconut soup all over South-East Asia. The best one I ever had was in Malacca where the famous walking canes come from. The dish looks a little complicated, but it is well worth the effort involved.

Total preparation/cooking time: 45 minutes
Serves 4

450g/1lb cooked free-range chicken, skinned, boned and chopped
3 tbsp oil, preferably peanut
225g/8oz pressed beancurd, cut into cubes
3 medium onions, peeled – one sliced finely and two diced finely
1 tsp finely chopped garlic
3 cashew nuts, grated or finely chopped
1 tbsp chopped green or red chillies
½ tsp shrimp paste
2 tsp ground cumin
1 tbsp ground coriander
1–2 tbsp *rempah*, or Malaysian red curry paste
1 litre/1¾pts thin coconut milk or dilute coconut cream with water
1 tbsp brown sugar
225g/8oz beansprouts, blanched
225g/8oz rice noodles, cooked at the very last minute
salt and freshly ground black pepper
1 tbsp chopped spring onions, some fresh coriander leaves, and 1 fresh red chilli, deseeded and chopped, to garnish

1 Heat 1 tbsp of the oil in a large pan and fry the beancurd until golden and crunchy on the outside then remove from the pan and keep warm.

2 Cook the sliced onion for about 5 minutes until golden and crispy then remove from the pan. Add another 1 tbsp of oil to the pan and cook the chopped onions and garlic for 2–3 minutes. Add the nuts, chillies, shrimp paste, cumin, coriander and *rempah* or curry paste. Stir well and cook over a medium heat for about 2 minutes. Then add the coconut milk, sugar and seasonings, bring to the boil and simmer for 10 minutes.

3 Heat the remaining oil in a frying pan or wok and stir-fry the chicken for 3–4 minutes. Add the beansprouts and stir-fry for 1–2 minutes, then remove and keep warm.

4 Divide the noodles between 4 deep bowls. Add some fried sliced onion to each one and top with the chicken, beansprouts and beancurd. Pour over the hot sauce. Garnish with the spring onions, coriander, basil, mint and chilli and serve.

Steamed rice with chicken and pork

These little bowls look splendid when turned out – with the rice at the bottom, topped with the chicken and pork. You could serve with a bowl of hot chillies if you're so inclined.

Total preparation/cooking time: 1 hour
plus soaking
Serves 4

450g/1lb Thai rice, thoroughly washed under running
    water and then left to soak in fresh, cold water for
    1 hour, then drained thoroughly
1 tbsp brown sugar
2½ tbsp light soy sauce
2 tbsp oyster sauce
225g/8oz free-range chicken breast fillets, skinned and
    cut into bite-size pieces
350g/12oz lean pork, diced
groundnut oil for frying
50g/2oz shiitake mushrooms, sliced
1 tbsp cornflour (optional)
salt and freshly ground black pepper
chopped fresh coriander leaves, to garnish

1 Put the sugar, soy sauce and oyster sauce into a bowl and mix together. Pour three-quarters of this mixture into a large bowl, add the chicken and pork and coat well.

2 Heat a little oil in a wok or large frying pan, add the chicken and pork and cook for about 5 minutes until golden. Add the mushrooms and a little water, then cover and simmer for about 20 minutes, until the pork and chicken are tender. If the sauce is very thin, mix the cornflour with a little water and add to the pan to thicken the sauce.

3 Mix the drained rice with the remaining soy sauce mixture and seasoning.

4 Put some chicken and pork mixture into the bottom of 4 heatproof bowls, and fill halfway with rice. Put the bowls into a bamboo steamer and set this on a rack in a large wok (or put them in a normal steamer). Steam over boiling water for about 30 minutes, keeping the water topped up, until the rice is cooked. Turn out and sprinkle with coriander leaves.

Stuffed quail, Turkish-style

Quail are tiny birds and, when boned and stuffed with rice,

walnuts and sultanas, two of them make a generous portion

for one person.

Total preparation/cooking time: 45 minutes

For each person
2 boned quail
6 vine leaves
1 tbsp sultanas
1 tbsp chopped walnuts
2 tbsp cooked rice (see below)
sea salt and freshly ground black pepper

1 Preheat the oven to 200°C/400°F/gas mark 6. Lay out the vine leaves and place one quail on top, skin-side down. Season with salt and pepper. Put the sultanas, walnuts and rice on top of the quail. Place the other quail on top and wrap in the vine leaves, leaving the legs protruding. Wrap in foil and seal both ends.

2 Bake in the oven for about 30 minutes.

Rice

olive oil
4 onions, finely chopped
6 cloves garlic, finely chopped
1kg/2¼lb long-grain rice, washed and drained
chicken stock
red chilli flakes
cinnamon

1 Heat the olive oil in a pan and fry the onions and garlic until soft. Add the rice and fry until translucent, then add enough chicken stock to cover the rice, cover the pan and cook gently for 6-8 minutes.

2 Add the chilli flakes and cinnamon to taste and cook for a further 2-3 minutes or until the rice is done. This dish can be eaten hot or cold.

Sautéed pheasant with calvados

Fruit and game are often cooked together, as here. If someone has given you a brace of pheasant, do check for lead shot.

Serves 2

2 pheasant breasts, on or off the bone depending
    on taste
1 apple
brown sugar, for sprinkling
25g/1oz butter
1 glass calvados
1 splash dry cider
1 tbsp apple sauce
170ml/6 fl oz chicken stock
170ml/6 fl oz double cream
salt and freshly ground black pepper

1 Peel, quarter and slice the apple. Sprinkle the slices with brown sugar and grill until brown. Set aside.

2 Fry the pheasant breasts in the butter on both sides until cooked.

3 Warm the calvados in a ladle, add to the pan and ignite. After about 15 seconds, if it is still burning, place the lid on the pan to kill the flame. Add a little cider and simmer for a minute or two. Remove the breasts and keep them warm while the sauce reduces.

4 As it reduces, add the apple sauce, chicken stock and cream. Season and stir, then continue simmering until you have a sauce consistency.

5 Place the breasts on a plate, dress with the sauce and garnish with the apple slices.

Roast grouse with wild mushrooms and red wine sauce
- the bed of roasting vegetables

Roast grouse with wild mushrooms and red wine sauce

Grouse have a dark flesh and a distinctive flavour, well matched
by this aromatic sauce.

Total preparation/cooking time: 55 minutes
Serves 1

1 whole, oven-ready grouse
butter, for frying
4 onions, roughly chopped
4 carrots, roughly chopped
4 sticks celery, roughly chopped
1 bulb garlic, cut in half horizontally
2 bay leaves
1 sprig thyme
1 sprig rosemary
1 standard measure whisky

For the sauce
butter, for frying
1 onion, roughly chopped
225g/8oz assorted wood mushrooms
300ml/½pt carton red wine sauce
salt and freshly ground black pepper

1 Preheat the oven to 200°C/400°F/gas mark 6.
Place the grouse on a bed of the onions, carrots,
celery, garlic, bay leaves, thyme and rosemary. Place
in the oven and cook for 35-40 minutes.

2 Remove the dish from the oven, place on the hob
and flame with the whisky. This helps release all the
juices from the wonderfully caramelised vegetables
and the grouse itself. Place the grouse on a serving
dish. Strain all the juices from the roasting dish and
set aside.

3 To make the sauce, heat the butter in a pan and,
when hot, fry the onion until lightly browned. Add the
mushrooms and cook gently. Add the reserved
roasting juices and the red wine sauce. Stir well and
simmer to reduce to a sauce consistency. Season to
taste and serve with the grouse.

Duck with kumquat and orange sauce

This dish is best made with a wild duck, but if you can't get one then use a farmed duck. Kumquats have a pleasant bitter-sweet flavour that is a perfect match for the richness of the duck.

Total preparation/cooking time: 45 minutes
Serves 1-2

1 whole, oven-ready duck
butter, for frying
4 onions, roughly chopped
4 carrots, roughly chopped
4 sticks celery, roughly chopped
1 bulb garlic, cut in half horizontally
2 bay leaves
1 sprig thyme
1 standard measure kirsch
1 glass white wine
180ml/6fl oz chicken stock
1 tbsp sugar
1 stick cinnamon
110g/4oz kumquats
1 knob butter
salt and freshly ground black pepper
1 orange, segmented, to garnish

1 Preheat the oven to 220°/425°F/gas mark 7. Heat the butter in a pan and fry the duck until browned all over, to seal it.

2 Sit the duck on a bed of the onions, carrots, celery, garlic, bay leaves and thyme in a flameproof dish and roast it for 30 minutes.

3 Remove the dish from the oven, place on the hob and flame with the kirsch. Place the duck on a serving dish.

4 Put the kirsch-scented meat juices in a smaller saucepan and add the white wine, chicken stock, sugar, cinnamon and kumquats. Reduce it down to a thicker consistency, about one-third its previous volume. Then add the knob of butter to give the sauce a lovely shine. Season to taste. Serve the duck with the sauce and garnish the plate with the orange segments.

Duck with kumquat and orange sauce – the kumquats add a bitter-sweet flavour

Rabbit stew

I like rabbit - although it's not very fashionable it's a lean meat with a superb flavour. The addition of the liver thickens and enriches the sauce.

Total preparation/cooking time: 1 hour 20 minutes
Serves 6

1 rabbit, jointed (retain the liver)
olive oil, for frying
flour, for coating
1 large splash sherry
4 onions, roughly chopped
6 small carrots, cleaned and chopped
2 sticks celery, roughly chopped
1 bulb fennel, cut into quarters
1 bottle Rioja wine
3 tbsp tomato purée
3 cloves garlic, peeled and crushed
salt and crushed peppercorns

1 Heat a little of the olive oil in a frying pan. Coat the rabbit joints in flour and fry in the oil until brown on all sides. Once the rabbit has browned, sprinkle with a little salt, add the sherry and reduce a little.

2 Meanwhile, heat some olive oil in a large pan and fry the onions, carrot, celery and fennel for about 3 minutes. Add the rabbit and sherry to the vegetables, pour in the wine and stir well.

3 Finely chop the rabbit liver and mix with the tomato purée, garlic and crushed peppercorns. Stir it into the pan to thicken and flavour the dish. Simmer, uncovered, for about an hour on a low heat.

Poacher's rabbit

And here's another rabbit dish I pulled out of the hat earlier! This is an Italian version.

Total preparation/cooking time: 1 hour
Serves 4

1 free-range rabbit with liver and kidneys, jointed in small pieces on the bone
6 tbsp olive oil
1 large onion, chopped
1 or 2 wineglasses of dry white wine
1 tbsp chopped fresh parsley
2 tbsp chopped capers
salt and freshly ground black pepper
chopped fresh parsley, to garnish

1 Heat 4 tbsp of the olive oil in a large pan and fry the onion gently for about 5 minutes, until softened. Add the rabbit joints with a good pinch of salt and fry for 5 minutes over a moderate heat, to brown them all over. Taste for seasoning. Cover the pan and cook for 20 minutes over a low heat – don't let the rabbit burn.

2 Add the glass (or two) of wine and continue to cook for about 20 minutes until the rabbit is tender. After 15 minutes, heat the remaining oil in a small frying pan. Quickly chop the liver and kidneys and sauté them briskly for 2 minutes. Add to the pan with the parsley, capers and more ground black pepper, bubble for a few moments and serve garnished with parsley.

Wild bear with berries on rosti

This is a dish I prepared one winter morning in the frozen wastes on the Swedish/Russian border, where bear is much esteemed. I include this recipe only as a bit of fun, but if for bear you read pork or veal and use redcurrants instead of lingonberries, you would have a delicious meal without the trouble of having to travel.

Total preparation/cooking time: 30 minutes
Serves 4

700g/1½lb bear loin (or beef, venison or marinated leg of pork), sliced into thin escalopes
a knob of butter
3 tbsp olive oil
a good splash of brandy or aquavit
200ml/7fl oz crème de cassis
300ml/½pt good beef stock
1 tbsp redcurrant jelly
110g/4oz lingonberries (or elderberries, redcurrants or blackcurrants)
salt and freshly ground black pepper

For the celeriac rosti
½ a celeriac, peeled and coarsely grated
1 large potato, peeled and coarsely grated
75g/3oz butter
1 tbsp olive oil
salt and freshly ground black pepper

1 Heat the butter and olive oil in a frying pan and fry the meat over a high heat. Season with salt, add the brandy or aquavit and set light to it. When the flames have subsided, add the crème de cassis. Remove the meat from the pan and keep warm.

2 Pour the stock into the pan, and whisk with the pan juices, and then add the redcurrant jelly and the berries. Season to taste with salt and plenty of pepper – the sauce should be quite spicy.

3 To make the rosti, put the celeriac and potato in a colander, rinse well then drain and pat dry. Melt half the butter and mix with the celeriac and potato, seasoning with salt and pepper, then shape into little mounds. Heat the remaining butter and the olive oil and fry the rosti for about 12 minutes or so, turning over once, until golden brown and crunchy. Serve with the meat and pour the sauce around.

Smoked pork in cherry sauce

For an easy red wine sauce, just add some stock and a little redcurrant jelly
to the pan juices once the meat has been removed and stir to thicken
slightly. Or buy one from your supermarket.

Total preparation/cooking time: 15 minutes
Serves 4

about 12–16 thin slices of smoked pork loin (weighing
    about 350–450g/12–16oz)
50g/2oz butter
2 shallots, finely chopped
2 tbsp cherry brandy or brandy
200ml/7fl oz bought red wine sauce (or see above)
150g/5oz stoned, fresh cherries
zest of 1 lemon, finely shredded
a few leaves of fresh thyme or lemon thyme
salt and freshly ground black pepper

1 Heat the butter in a frying pan and add the pork loin
slices. Sauté them lightly for about a minute on each
side and then add the chopped shallots and cook for
about 5 minutes until slightly browned. Pour in the
cherry brandy or brandy and set light to it. When the
flames have died down, remove the meat from the pan,
place on a serving dish and keep in a warm place.

2 Add the red wine sauce to the pan and stir
everything together; then add the cherries. Heat for a
few moments, and add the lemon zest and thyme
leaves. Check the seasoning, pour the sauce over the
meat and serve.

Smoked pork in cherry sauce –
quick, simple and delicious

Ham with Chablis and mustard sauce – try to use the very best quality ham

Ham with Chablis and mustard sauce

First find a butcher who cooks good-quality ham on the bone and ask him for 4 or 6 generous slices of it. This dish really won't come off with those little square, plastic packs of cooked ham.

Serve with fresh pasta noodles (not the traditional accompaniment, but they go brilliantly with this dish) and a really crisp, mixed leaf salad. So, the rest of the ingredients then!

Total preparation/cooking time: 1 hour
Serves 4–6

6 generous slices of cooked, slightly smoked ham, off
    the bone if possible (unsmoked ham is also OK)
100g/3½oz butter
dash of olive oil
225g/8oz button mushrooms, very finely sliced
3 or 4 shallots, very finely diced
a bottle of good white Burgundy or Chablis
about 150ml/¼pt chicken stock
1 tbsp smooth Dijon mustard
1 tbsp grainy Dijon-style mustard
100ml/3½fl oz double cream
a good knob of butter
salt and freshly ground black pepper

1 Heat half the butter and the olive oil in a heavy frying pan and cook the mushrooms and shallots until the shallots are golden and just beginning to caramelise lightly. Add the white wine, which should be chilled (because hopefully you have a glass in your hand at the same time), turn up the heat and reduce the liquid by half.

2 Add the chicken stock, bring to a bubble, and cook for 3-4 minutes. Reduce the heat to a simmer and gently stir in both mustards so as not to damage the mushrooms. Now taste it to see how strong it is, then stir in the cream gently over a low heat, taste and season with salt and pepper. If the sauce is a little too thin, reduce gently and carefully stir in some little knobs of butter that will amalgamate, thicken and enrich the sauce.

3 While the sauce is cooking, heat the remaining butter and oil in a pan and quickly fry the ham slices on both sides. Place on a serving dish, pour the sauce over the ham and serve.

Barbecued pork chops

Almost anywhere in Spain, you will find excellent pork chops. They are invariably cooked over a charcoal fire and served simply or indeed they are whacked onto a *plancha*, which as you know is a heated metal plate. They are often served with a fried egg on top and served with super chips. I am assuming that you are going to cook this on the barbecue.

Total preparation/cooking time: 15 minutes
    plus marinating
Serves 4

Get some really good, thin pork chops and marinate them in a mixture of olive oil, finely chopped garlic, a pinch of paprika, a squeeze of lemon juice, a little salt and some freshly ground black pepper.

Leave them in the marinade, turning them from time to time, for a couple of hours. Then make sure your barbecue is really hot, whack on the chops and cook them.

Czech pork and liver balls

Caul, which holds the meatballs together, looks like a hairnet. Order it from your butcher.

Total preparation/cooking time: 1¼ hours
Serves 6

900g/2lb belly pork, minced
225g/8oz pork liver, minced
110g/4oz fresh white breadcrumbs
1 onion, finely chopped
1 bunch fresh sage, chopped
1 bunch fresh parsley, chopped
1 tbsp dried mixed herbs
450g/1lb pork caul

For the gravy
1 knob butter
3 onions, finely sliced
1 glass red wine
150ml/¼pt brown stock
1 tbsp tomato purée
salt and freshly ground black pepper

1 Preheat the oven to 180°C/350°F/gas mark 4. Mix the minced pork and liver with the breadcrumbs, onion, sage, parsley and dried herbs. Once thoroughly mixed, form into balls about the size of a cricket ball. Wrap the balls in the caul and place them on a baking tray with a little water to help them steam. Place in the oven and cook for 50 minutes.

2 Towards the end of the cooking time, make the gravy. Heat some butter in a pan and fry the onions until soft and browned. Add the red wine, some pepper and the stock, then add the tomato purée and whisk in as it heats through. Simmer gently for a few minutes until thoroughly heated.

3 Serve the pork and liver balls in the gravy.

Poached pork in cabbage

Pork and apples are a terrific combination, and this dish is perfect for a bit of self-indulgence.

Total preparation/cooking time: 1¼ hours
Serves 6

900g/2lb belly pork, minced
2 medium eggs
240ml/8fl oz fresh double cream
4 tomatoes, deseeded and diced
1 tbsp dried mixed herbs
110g/4oz fresh white breadcrumbs
½ tbsp paprika
1 tbsp tomato purée
1 bunch fresh parsley, chopped
2 fresh red chillies, finely diced
2 cloves garlic, crushed
outer green leaves of 1 savoy cabbage
3.5 litres/6pts good pork or chicken stock

For the sauce
oil, for frying
1 large onion, chopped
6 apples, peeled, cored and roughly chopped (not too
    small)
1 measure brandy
1 glass white wine
½ tbsp paprika
1 knob butter

1 Whisk the eggs and then add 2 tbsp of the cream, the tomatoes, pork, herbs, breadcrumbs, paprika, tomato purée, parsley, chillies and garlic.

2 Lay clingfilm on a work surface and on top of this make a square of the cabbage leaves so they overlap in the centre. Put the meat mixture in the centre and wrap the leaves around it to reform the shape of the cabbage. Tightly wrap it in the cling film.

3 Bring the stock to the boil in a large saucepan. Put the clingfilm-wrapped cabbage ball into the pan and cover with a lid. Gently simmer for about 1 hour.

4 To make the sauce, heat the oil and fry the onion with the chopped apple. Add the brandy and white wine, let that reduce by about two thirds, to a sauce consistency and then add the paprika. Now add the remaining cream and to thicken, a knob of butter whisking all the time. Pour over the cabbage ball and serve.

Sausage and pepper macaroni
- extremely tasty

Sausage and pepper macaroni

This couldn't be simpler to make and is extremely tasty.

Total preparation/cooking time: 30 minutes
Serves 4

225g/8oz cooked macaroni
3 tbsp olive oil
1 onion, finely chopped
1 large green pepper, cored, deseeded and finely
 chopped
2 cloves garlic, finely chopped
4 tomatoes, skinned and finely chopped
110g/4oz *serrano* ham, diced
3 chorizo sausages, thinly sliced
110g/4oz manchego or Cheddar cheese, grated
freshly ground black pepper

1 Heat the olive oil in a frying pan and sauté the
onion, pepper, garlic and tomatoes until you have a
rich sauce. Add the ham and sausage to heat through
and season with black pepper. If the sauce is a little
dry add a dash of water.

2 Preheat the grill. Stir the sausage mixture into the
cooked macaroni, transfer to a gratin dish and sprinkle
the surface liberally with grated cheese. Grill for a few
minutes until the cheese has melted, then serve.

Stir-fried beef with cashew nuts

On Ko Samui, that beautiful island in the Gulf of Thailand, cashew nuts grow in profusion, although, did you know, that the cashew tree grows a kind of an apple and on the bottom of each apple is just one cashew nut. That's why they are so expensive. And, for your further edification, in Goa, India, after they have harvested the cashew nut, they use the apple to make a kind of a cider that they then distil into the most diabolical, but magnificent, alcohol.

Total preparation/cooking time: 20 minutes
Serves 4

450g/1lb lean beef, such as fillet, thinly sliced and
　　cut into strips (or of course you can use pork,
　　chicken, prawns or whatever)
2 tbsp groundnut or sesame oil
1 onion, halved and sliced
1 clove garlic, finely chopped
2.5cm/1in piece fresh root ginger, finely chopped
　　or grated
1 tsp brown sugar
2 tbsp light soy sauce
3 spring onions, sliced diagonally
1 small green and 1 small red pepper, deseeded and
　　thinly sliced lengthways
2 stalks celery, chopped to the same size as the spring
　　onions
6 pieces dried Chinese black mushrooms, soaked,
　　drained and chopped
4 tbsp roasted cashew nuts
a dash of beef stock
ground white pepper
celery leaves, to garnish

1 Heat the oil in a wok or frying pan. Add the onion, garlic and ginger and stir-fry over a high heat for 2-3 minutes. Add the beef and stir-fry for a further 2-3 minutes, until browned. Season to taste with the sugar, soy sauce and pepper.

2 Add the spring onions, green and red peppers, celery, mushrooms and nuts. Pour in a little beef stock and stir-fry for about 3 minutes. Garnish with celery leaves, and serve with white rice noodles.

Stir-fried beef with cashew nuts – full of different textures and flavours

Malaysian beef rendang

The curry is sour, dry, hot, and scrumptious. In street stalls, hotels and restaurants it is served all day, so you can have it for breakfast, which, if you've woken with a sore head, makes a brilliant hangover cure. Serve with a pineapple, chilli and cucumber salad and coconut rice.

Total preparation/cooking time: 1¼ hours
Serves 8–10

1.4kg/3lb brisket of beef, cut into large chunks
nut oil for frying
a dash of tamarind concentrate
350ml/12fl oz coconut cream
a few lime leaves
juice of 1 or 2 lemons
salt and freshly ground black pepper

For the Rendang curry paste
6–8 red chillies, deseeded and finely chopped
6 shallots, finely chopped
2 or 3 cloves garlic, finely chopped
1 tbsp ground turmeric
1 stalk lemon grass, chopped

1 To make the curry paste, blend all the ingredients in a food processor to make a smooth paste, adding a little water if necessary (or lazy people can buy Malaysian red curry paste in jars from shops).

2 Heat the nut oil in a pan and brown the beef on all sides. Lower the heat and stir in the Rendang curry paste. When the meat is well coated with the paste, stir in all the other ingredients and simmer slowly, for about an hour, until the beef is tender and the sauce is quite dry.

Thai green beef curry

Those of you familiar with Thai food know it can be pretty hot. The curry paste in this beef curry is powerful but the coconut milk tames it to a certain extent. You can of course buy Thai green curry paste, but if you wish to make your own use the ingredients opposite.

Total preparation/cooking time: 20 minutes
Serves 3–4

350g/12oz fillet of beef, thinly sliced and then cut into
    strips (or chicken, pork or prawns)
nut oil for frying
3–4 tbsp green curry paste (see right)
400ml/14fl oz coconut cream
2 tbsp fish sauce
1 tbsp brown sugar
1 aubergine, peeled, cut into 12mm/½in cubes and
    quickly blanched and strained
1 cup of frozen green peas
2 green tomatoes, deseeded and coarsely chopped
1 heaped tsp fresh green peppercorns, or preserved
    canned green peppercorns rinsed in fresh water
2.5cm/1in fresh root ginger, chopped
3–4 lime leaves, chopped
fresh basil leaves

1 Heat the nut oil in a large pan, add the beef and stir-fry over a high heat for a minute or two. Then stir in the green curry paste and cook for a minute or two.

2 Add the coconut cream, fish sauce and sugar and bring to the boil, stirring all the time. Reduce the heat, add all the remaining ingredients, give it a quick stir and serve, garnished with the basil leaves.

For the green curry paste

10-12 deseeded red chillies, 6 cloves garlic, 2-3 tbsp finely chopped onion, 1 tbsp chopped lemon grass, 1 tbsp chopped fresh root ginger, 1 tbsp chopped fresh coriander, a dash of shrimp paste, a couple of good pinches of ground cumin, salt and 3 tbsp groundnut oil – whiz all of these together in a food processor to make a paste. Keep in the fridge until needed. (For red curry paste, substitute red chillies for green.)

Beef vindaloo

Vindaloo was created in the Portuguese/Indian colony of Goa and it takes its name from the Portuguese influence in Goan cooking, vin (literally wine or vinegar in Portuguese) and aloo (the Indian for potato), and it is the easiest thing in the world to cook! Although in Goa, pork is more often used than beef.

Total preparation/cooking time: 45 minutes
Serves 4

about 800g/1¾ lb diced beef
vegetable or coconut oil
2 red onions, finely chopped
3 or 4 medium potatoes, peeled and cut into fairly large
    cubes
sugar
salt

For the masala
1 tsp cumin seeds
1 tsp black peppercorns
1 tsp ground turmeric
3 or 4 cloves
2 cinnamon sticks
about 15 dried red chillies
4 fresh green chillies
a large knob fresh root ginger, peeled
red wine vinegar

1 To make the masala, blend all the ingredients together, adding enough vinegar to make a smooth paste.

2 Heat the oil in a large pan and sauté the onions until softened. Stir in the masala paste and cook for a minute or so then stir in the meat and continue to cook for a few minutes until the meat and masala have amalgamated. Add enough water to make a rich, fairly thick gravy and simmer gently until the meat is about half cooked.

3 Add the potato cubes and season with a little sugar and salt and continue cooking until the meat is tender and the potatoes are cooked. The gravy should be a natural, rich red colour, although in some parts of the world, vindaloos are, quite improperly, artificially coloured, as indeed are many tandooris.

Dynamite chilli beef –
for lovers of chilli

Dynamite chilli beef

A truly fiery creation of my chum Chom, *la maîtresse de la cuisine* at the Tongsai Bay Hotel, in Ko Samui, this dish takes its name from the small, very hot chillies known as bird's-eye or dynamite chillies. Serve on a bed of steamed rice.

Total preparation/cooking time: 20 minutes
Serves 4

700g/1½lb fillet steak, finely sliced
2 shallots, chopped
2.5cm/1in piece galangal, chopped (galangal is a Thai
    variety of ginger so you can of course use ginger
    instead)
2 cloves garlic
2 chillies (preferably bird's-eye), deseeded and chopped
whisky, to flame
2 tbsp groundnut oil
a few fresh green peppercorns
1 red and 1 green chilli, deseeded and sliced lengthways
2–3 lime leaves, torn
110g/4oz green beans, cut into 2.5cm/1in lengths
1 tbsp fish sauce
1 tsp demerara sugar
2 tsp white distilled vinegar or rice vinegar
small handful fresh basil leaves, to garnish

1 Whiz the shallots, galangal, garlic and chillies together to a smooth paste.

2 Heat the oil in a frying pan or wok and stir-fry the beef. Flame with whisky then stir in the garlic mixture and cook for a few moments.

3 Add the peppercorns, chillies, lime leaves and green beans. Stir-fry over a high heat for about 5 minutes. The vegetables should still be crisp and bright coloured. Pop in the fish sauce, brown sugar and vinegar and mix well. Garnish with basil leaves and serve with rice.

Salmon baked in filo pastry, stuffed with crystallised ginger, sultanas and lime

Although this dish takes a little longer than most to cook, it couldn't be simpler to make – and it looks jolly impressive.

Total preparation/cooking time: 1 hour
    10 minutes
Serves 10

1 salmon, skinned, filleted and boned
1 packet filo pastry
225g/8oz butter, melted
1 tbsp crystallised ginger
110g/4oz mixed sultanas
2 limes, sliced
1 tbsp parsley, chopped
50g/2oz butter, softened
juice of 1 lemon
1 egg beaten with a splash of milk, for egg wash
flour, for dusting
salt and freshly ground black pepper

1 Preheat the oven to 190˚C/375˚F/gas mark 5. Arrange the sheets of filo pastry to form a square, large enough to wrap round the salmon. Brush well with some of the melted butter.

2 Put one of the salmon fillets in the middle of the pastry square, so that the pastry can be folded over. Spread the ginger, sultanas and slices of lime in a layer all over the top of the fillet and sprinkle with the parsley, knobs of butter and some seasoning. Put the other salmon fillet on the top of the first and sprinkle with lemon juice and a little more salt and pepper. Brush more melted butter on the pastry all around the fish, then wrap the filo pastry around the fish to form a parcel.

3 Brush the whole of the pastry case with egg wash (to get a nice golden colour when cooked), pop it in the oven and bake for 50 minutes.

Salmon baked in filo pastry, stuffed with crystallised ginger, sultanas and lime – looks jolly impressive

Dublin Bay prawns in a champagne sauce

Fresh truffles are vastly superior to preserved, but if you can't get them, canned or bottled will do; add the juices to the stock. You can buy ready-made fish stock from the supermarket, if you don't have any to hand.

Total preparation/cooking time: 30 minutes
Serves 4 as a main course, 8 as a starter

2kg/4½lb large Dublin Bay prawns, shelled
olive oil and butter for frying
4 garlic cloves, finely chopped
5 shallots, finely chopped
1 glass of Marc de Champagne or Cognac
a dash of fish stock (buy from the supermarket)
a glass or two of Champagne
300ml/½pt double cream
2 or 3 black truffles, finely sliced
a large pinch of saffron stamens
a knob of butter
salt and freshly ground black pepper
a handful of finely chopped parsley, to garnish

1 Heat the olive oil and butter in a large sauté pan, add the garlic and shallots and cook until soft. Now add the prawns, turning them in the pan until they start to turn red, then add the Cognac and flame. Add the fish stock and Champagne, bring to the boil and simmer for 2 or 3 minutes until the prawns are completely red, then remove them and keep them warm while finishing the sauce.

2 Over a high heat, reduce the liquid in the pan by half, then lower the heat and whisk in the cream, the truffles, saffron and salt and pepper. Finally work in the knob of butter to produce a smooth, thin, custard-like sauce. Return the prawns to the sauce to warm through, sprinkle with parsley and serve.

Hong Kong-style sweet and sour prawns

If you're short on time but want to cook up something special, try this tasty number that I've adapted from one I cooked while out in Hong Kong.

Total preparation/cooking time: 20 minutes
Serves 4

450g/1lb raw tiger prawns, shelled, deveined and tails left intact
groundnut or sunflower oil
1 red chilli, deseeded and finely sliced
2 red peppers, deseeded and finely sliced
6 spring onions, cut into approx. 2.5cm/1in batons
a dash of rice wine or dry sherry
225ml/8fl oz ready-prepared sweet and sour sauce – buy it from the supermarket
salt and freshly ground black pepper
a bunch of fresh coriander, chopped, to garnish

1 Slash along the back of each prawn, so that when you fry them they will open up like butterflies – very pretty.

2 Heat a couple of tablespoons of oil in a wok or frying pan. Stir-fry the chillies, peppers and spring onions together for 2–3 minutes. Add the prawns and stir-fry. Tip in the rice wine or sherry and set fire to it. Let it bubble away to almost nothing then stir in the sweet and sour sauce. Season with salt and pepper.

3 Garnish with chopped coriander and serve with rice. And there you have the perfect cheat's, instant Hong Kong-style stir-fry.

Mussel curry with pineapple

My chum Chom really loves these fiery dishes (see Dynamite chilli beef, page 107), and this is another of his creations. Excellent for brunch to really wake up your system.

Total preparation/cooking time: 40 minutes
Serves 2–3

700g/1½lb mussels in shells
1 pineapple, cut in half lengthways
7.5cm/3in piece galangal or ginger, finely chopped
2 stalks lemon grass, finely chopped
a handful basil sprigs
groundnut oil
1 tbsp red curry paste (see page 104)
1 tbsp fish sauce
4 tbsp coconut cream
1 tsp palm or demerara sugar
4 lime leaves, torn into pieces
2 red chillies, deseeded and cut into thin strips
    lengthways

1 Wash and scrub the mussels thoroughly in cold water, and remove beards and barnacles. Discard any that are open. Hollow out the pineapple halves, reserving the 'shells'. Discard the pineapple core and chop the flesh into small pieces.

2 Put the mussels, galangal, lemon grass and basil into a large pan and add water to a depth of 12mm/½in. Cover the pan, bring to the boil and cook for 5-10 minutes, shaking the pan frequently, until the mussels have opened. Discard any that remain closed. Remove the mussels from their shells and pop them into the pineapple shells.

3 Heat the oil in a pan or wok and cook the red curry paste for a minute then gently stir in the fish sauce, coconut cream, brown sugar, lime leaves and chillies. Add the chopped pineapple and heat through for a minute or two. Pour over the mussels in the pineapple shells and serve.

Oriental lobster in black bean sauce - the only way to eat this is with your fingers

Oriental lobster in black bean sauce

Ready-cooked lobsters are available in supermarkets, so for the squeamish among you there's no need to go through the business of despatching a live one. But of course the dish won't be quite as good.

Total preparation/cooking time: 25 minutes
Serves 1–2

1 fresh lobster about 900 g/2lb, washed and cut into
    small pieces, shell left on
1 tbsp ginger wine or dry sherry
1 tbsp cornflour
1 litre/1¾pts oil, for deep frying
2 green peppers, deseeded and cut into 1cm/½ in
    squares
3 red chillies, deseeded and thinly sliced
1 tsp minced root ginger
2 cloves garlic, minced or finely chopped
2 tbsp preserved black bean paste
1 tsp rice wine or dry sherry
120ml/4fl oz fish or vegetable stock
3 tbsp light soy sauce
3 tsp sugar
2 spring onions, sliced
freshly ground black pepper

1 Mix together the ginger wine or sherry, cornflour and a large pinch of pepper. Coat the lobster pieces with this mixture.

2 Reserve 3 tbsp of the oil and heat the remaining oil in a large pan. Deep-fry the lobster pieces for 1-2 minutes, then lift out and drain. Heat the remaining 3 tbsp oil in a wok or frying pan and sauté the green peppers, chillies, ginger and garlic for a couple of minutes. Stir in the black bean paste and mix well.

3 Return the lobster pieces to the pan with the wine or sherry, stock and seasonings. Cover and simmer for 2-5 minutes. Finally, toss in the spring onions and serve.

Black seafood risotto

Try not to get the squid ink on your hands or clothes – it stains!

Total preparation/cooking time: 25 minutes
Serves 6

180ml/6fl oz olive oil, for frying
2 onions, chopped
1kg/2¼lb short-grain rice
450g/1lb tomatoes, chopped
4 cloves garlic, crushed
1 bottle white wine, or 1.2 litres/2pts fish stock if preferred
6 sachets squid ink
1kg/2¼lb seafood (such as prepared squid, prawns, cockles, mussels)

1 Heat the olive oil in a large pan and add the onion and rice. Stir to ensure the rice is coated in the oil. Add the tomatoes and garlic and cook gently for 2–3 minutes.

2 Add the wine or fish stock, bring to a simmer, replace the lid and cook for a further 10 minutes.

3 Add the squid ink, stir well and then add the seafood. Replace the lid for 5 minutes until the seafood is cooked, then serve.

Floyd's paella

Do use the best-quality Spanish short grain rice and first-quality olive oil for this dish, and saffron stamens – not the powdered stuff. A 50cm/20in paella tin will cook enough for about 10 people, and you will need the following ingredients:

Total preparation/cooking time: 55 minutes
Serves 10

olive oil
1 small chicken, cut into bite-sized pieces, bones and all
2 large onions, finely chopped
6 cloves of garlic, finely chopped
1kg/2¼lb Spanish short-grain rice, washed, rinsed, drained and dried
2 red peppers, chopped
6 large tomatoes, skinned, deseeded and chopped
2 bay leaves
2 sprigs of fresh thyme
a large pinch saffron
fish or chicken stock to cover
1kg/2¼lb mussels and/or clams, cleaned, debearded and rinsed
1kg/2¼lb frozen petits pois
500g/1lb 2 oz fresh prawns in their shells
sea salt and freshly ground black pepper

1 Heat some olive oil in a very large pan and fry the chicken until it is crisp on the outside. Then add the onions, garlic and rice and stir around until each grain is coated with oil. Season with salt and pepper.

2 Stir in the red peppers and tomatoes. Add the bay leaves, thyme and saffron and pour in enough stock or water to cover the rice. Cover and cook gently until all the liquid has been absorbed. At this point, the rice will not be quite cooked.

3 Add the mussels and/or clams, the frozen peas and the prawns to the pan and replace the lid. When the mussels and/or clams have opened the dish is ready. Discard any that don't open.

Spanish fish pie

The Spanish use fish complete with bones and skin in this dish. However, I think it is much kinder to your family and friends to use thick fillets of any firm-fleshed white fish, free of bone and skin. Serve with a green salad.

Total preparation/cooking time: 45 minutes
Serves 4

4 x 175g/6oz firm-fleshed white fish fillets e.g. hake,
    monkfish, cod etc.
150ml/5fl oz olive oil
450g/1lb potatoes, very thinly sliced, rinsed and dried
2 medium onions, very, very, very finely sliced
25g/1oz plain flour
3 cloves garlic, finely chopped
1 tbsp paprika
300ml/½pt fresh tomato sauce (buy a jar from the
    supermarket)
1 glass dry white wine
Pernod, Pastis or Ricard
3–4 handfuls of fresh white breadcrumbs
salt and freshly ground black pepper

1 In a very large frying pan heat the olive oil and stir-fry the potatoes for about 30 seconds. Remove them, and do the same with the onion. Remove them. Dredge the fish fillets in the flour then fry in the oil for about half a minute on each side. Turn off the heat.

2 Preheat the oven to 190°C/375°F/gas mark 5. Stir the garlic and paprika into the tomato sauce. Now get a large gratin dish and put the fish in first, then the onions, then the potatoes and then the fresh tomato sauce. Add a dash of wine and a dash of Pernod, Pastis or Ricard, season with salt and pepper, cover with breadcrumbs and shake over a little olive oil. Bake for 30–40 minutes.

Barbecued whole fish with a pineapple and ginger hot salsa

Total preparation/cooking time: 30 minutes

While I was filming *Floyd on Africa*, many years ago, I spent a wonderful morning fishing on the Zambezi River, and to my delight and amazement, I caught a wonderful Tiger Fish, which is a bit like a perch in flavour. So the director asked me to cook it and make a sauce. I had very limited equipment – a little clay pot with some charcoal in it and a simple camping gaz burner.

First I rummaged in my ice box and found I had a few bits and pieces and my bits and pieces were some chopped onions, some chopped tomatoes, some chopped chillies, red and green, some chopped ginger, and a few cubes of chopped pineapple. I had some oil, so I heated the oil and stir-fried all of the above. Unbelievably I seemed to have a bottle of sherry, so I moistened the stir-fry with a dash of sherry, then in one of my pockets I found a bottle of soy sauce, so I added a dash of that, and then at the bottom of the icebox I found some coriander and some chives, which I chopped and stirred into my little sauce. I didn't need to keep the sauce warm, because it was so hot – 45˚F I think, so it stayed warm while I seasoned my fish with salt and pepper and lemon juice and barbecued it.

After it was cooked, I skinned it and poured over the still warm sauce. So, if one fine summer's day you decide to put some trout, bream, perch or salmon steaks on the barbecue in your summery garden, first make this little sauce!

Barbecued whole fish with
a pineapple and ginger hot salsa -
first catch your fish!

Roast monkfish

I know monkfish is more expensive than fillet steak, but when you want to treat yourself you can't go wrong with this truly impressive dish.

Total preparation/cooking time: 55 minutes
Serves 4–6

900g/2lb monkfish tail, skinned
lemon juice
1 tbsp parsley, finely chopped
2 cloves garlic, very finely chopped
knob of butter
8 small whole onions, sautéed in butter until golden
2oz/50g smoked bacon, diced
1 glass dry white wine
150ml/¼pt double cream
salt and freshly ground black pepper

1 Preheat the oven to 200°C/400°F/gas mark 6. Run a knife lengthways through the fish and remove the single backbone. Season both fillets with salt and pepper and lemon juice and sprinkle the parsley and garlic on top of one of the fillets. Place the other fillet on top and, using several little pieces of string, tie the fish back together into its original shape.

2 Butter a roasting tray and put the fish on it with the onions and bacon. Place in the oven and cook for 30 minutes. Add the wine to the roasting tray, turn the fish over and cook for a further 15 minutes or so. Remove the fish, onions and bacon to a warm serving dish.

3 Over a low heat, stir the cream into the juices in the roasting pan. Strain the sauce over the fish and serve. Carve as you would a leg of lamb, in slices.

Stir-fried scallops with peppers and spring onions

I think scallops are brilliant – that is, as long as you don't overcook them. Make sure they go into a really hot pan to sear them.

Total preparation/cooking time: 15 minutes
Serves 1–2

6 fresh, prepared scallops
1 tbsp vegetable oil
1 tbsp shredded, deseeded red chilli
1 tbsp finely chopped garlic
1 tbsp finely chopped fresh root ginger
50g/2oz green peppers, deseeded and cut into 12mm/½in pieces
1 tbsp shredded carrot
4 spring onions, cut into 2.5cm/1in pieces
dash of dark soy sauce

1 Heat the oil in a wok or frying pan and sear the scallops for around 3-4 minutes, until they become opaque and slightly golden, then remove.

2 Throw the chillies, garlic, ginger, green peppers, carrot and spring onions into the wok or pan and stir-fry for 5 seconds over a high heat. Replace the scallops. Stir briefly and add the soy sauce. Toss well together and serve.

Squid and pepper stir-fry

In about 1995, shortly after Nelson Mandela became president of South Africa, I made an unforgettable journey to that fabulous country, famous for rugby, barbecues (known as bries) and really quite drinkable wine. I stayed in an absolutely splendid hotel in Plettenburg Bay while I was filming *Floyd on Africa*, a BBC TV series. One morning, we decided to go squid fishing, or rather we took a power boat out to the squid fishing fleet where the locals were hand-lining for the said squid, and in the way of television programmes, I was required to set up my gas burner and a wok and cook the catch. Well, I also nearly cooked the boat because the gas bottle exploded and the deck caught fire. However, being good boy scouts we continued as if nothing had happened.

The strange thing is, though, that our Mr. Fixit said that in order to keep the boys happily fishing, you would have to buy them some more ice cream. Ice cream is a euphemism or a code word for marijuana! Without which they would not, or could not, endure several days trapped on a 40 foot boat working themselves to death. This is what I cooked on their boat.

Total preparation/cooking time: 15 minutes
Serves 4

450g/1lb fresh squid, sliced into rings
3–4 tbsp olive oil
2 onions, finely chopped
1 red pepper, cut into julienne strips
1 green pepper, cut into julienne strips
5 tomatoes, skinned, deseeded and diced
3 dried red chillies, chopped
4 garlic cloves, finely sliced
large handful of spinach leaves, chard or similar greens,
   well washed and drained
salt and freshly ground black pepper
4 tbsp soy sauce

1 Heat the olive oil in a wok until very hot. Add the squid and onions and stir-fry for about 30 seconds. Then add the peppers and stir-fry for a further minute. Add the tomatoes, chillies and garlic and cook for another minute or so.

2 At the last minute stir in the leaves. Season, then sprinkle with soy sauce, toss and serve.

Steamed scallops

The colours of the various ingredients in the scallop shells are superb. It's

fresh, light and delicious.

Total preparation/cooking time: 20 minutes
Serves 4

4 scallop shells, cleaned
8 fresh scallops
110g/4oz young spinach leaves
1 leek, finely shredded
1 tsp ginger, shredded
1 red pepper, finely sliced
1 green pepper, finely sliced
2 cloves garlic, finely chopped
4 spring onions, chopped
4 basil leaves
2 tomatoes, skinned, deseeded and diced

1 Take the cleaned scallop shells and arrange 4 or 5 whole spinach leaves in each. Add some of the leek, ginger, red and green peppers, garlic, spring onions and tomato and top with 2 scallops and a basil leaf in each.

2 Place the shells in a steamer, replace the lid and cook for 8 minutes. Remove from the steamer and serve in their shells.

Pan-fried scallops with leek and potato cakes

A simple dish but extremely tasty.

Total preparation/cooking time: 40 minutes
Serves 4

8 large fresh scallops
900g/2lb potatoes, quartered
175g/6oz butter
110ml/4fl oz double cream
1 egg, beaten
1 leek, very finely chopped
175g/6oz bacon lardons, cooked
oil and butter, for frying
olive oil, for searing
juice of 1 lemon
half bunch chives, finely chopped

1 Cook the potatoes and drain. Mash with 50g/2oz of the butter, the cream and the egg. Add the leek and bacon lardons and mix well. Form into four large potato cakes. Heat the butter and oil in a pan until hot, then fry the potato cakes until golden brown.

2 Put the olive oil in another pan and, when hot, sear the scallops. Then heat through gently until cooked.

3 Heat the remaining butter in a pan and whisk in the lemon juice until thoroughly amalgamated, then stir in the chives. Pour the sauce over the cooked scallops, and serve with the potato cakes.

Steamed scallops – the raw ingredients

Scallops and beans with pasta – an unusual
combination that really works

Scallops and beans with pasta

The Parma ham gives a great flavour to this little dish, and goes brilliantly
with the sweet taste of the scallops.

Total preparation/cooking time: 20 minutes
Serves 4

12-16 fresh scallops (depending on their size), removed
    from their shells and washed
olive oil
about 50g/2oz fatty Parma ham, diced into small cubes,
    or smoked lardons
225g/8oz fresh tagliatelle
450g/1lb fresh young broad beans, shelled, blanched
    briefly in boiling water and peeled
juice of ½ lemon
110g/4oz rocket or young spinach leaves, rinsed
75g/3oz cherry tomatoes, quartered
salt and freshly ground black pepper

1 Heat some olive oil in a large frying pan. Add the
ham or lardons and fry them until crispy. In the
meantime, cook the pasta in a large pan of lightly
salted boiling water for 4–5 minutes, until it is just
tender. Drain the pasta, place in a serving dish and
keep warm.

2 Add the scallops to the ham or lardons and stir-fry
them for a minute or two, then add the broad beans
and continue to stir-fry then season with salt, pepper
and lemon juice. Once cooked tip them on top of the
pasta.

3 Heat a little olive oil in the frying pan and quickly
stir-fry the rocket or spinach. Mix into the pasta and
scallops, scatter some halved cherry tomatoes over
the top and serve.

Desserts and Drinks

A confession I must make is that whereas elsewhere in this book I protested that I was not a glutton, I do have a very sweet tooth and very often, in some exquisite restaurant, where they have a really fine pâtissière, I will often just have an hors d'oeuvre followed by a couple of puddings. I am equally happy spooning out a wonderful raspberry soufflé in somewhere like the Gavroche or buying a slice of mango sprinkled with crushed, dried red chillies from a street hawker in Bangkok, but I must confess, I don't really have the patience, or indeed the hands, to be a first-class pudding cook. And this little selection is some of my favourite puddings from my own, admittedly, rather small, but refreshingly delicious repertoire.

Floating islands

This is one of my favourite desserts - soft meringues poached in custard. If you have the time and the inclination, the almond praline is brilliant with this dish.

Total preparation/cooking time: 30 minutes plus chilling (without praline)
Serves 4

300ml/½pt milk
300ml/½pt single cream
3 eggs, separated
150g/5oz caster sugar

For the garnish
soft caramel or powdered almond praline

1 Put the milk and cream and 75g/3oz of the caster sugar into a pan and bring very slowly to the simmer. Whisk the egg whites until they form stiff white peaks, then whisk in the rest of the caster sugar until the mixture is very shiny and stiff.

2 With a small dessertspoon, form little balls of meringue and poach them in the cream and milk for 2 to 3 minutes, or until they have swollen to approximately double their size. Strain them on kitchen paper and repeat the procedure until you have used up all the meringue.

3 Whisk the egg yolks and pour into the milk and cream mixture, whisking all the time over a low heat until the custard thickens slightly. Do not boil.
Strain the custard through a sieve into a serving dish, float the islands on top and chill.

4 Once the rest of the dish is completed and has chilled, make the caramel. Simmer 200g/7oz caster sugar and 500ml/2fl oz water until you have a light brown caramel. Pour it over the islands and custard in a thin stream - it will set and be crunchy - and serve.
If you are making the praline, put 150g/5oz coarsely chopped unblanched almonds into a pan with 150g/5oz sugar and cook gently until the sugar melts and begins to caramelise. Immediately pour it onto a piece of greaseproof paper and leave to set. When it is cold, whiz it up briefly in a food processor and sprinkle it over the cooled finished dish.

Floyd's instant gratin of summer fruits

Total preparation/cooking time: 10 minutes
Serves 4

2 cartons fresh custard
small tub of crème fraîche
vanilla-flavoured caster sugar (you can put a couple of
    pods into a sealed jar and leave for a few days, always
    useful to keep in the cupboard)
selection of soft fruits, e.g. raspberries, quartered
    strawberries, sliced kiwi fruit, sliced peach, peeled,
    deseeded, halved grapes, etc.

1 Preheat the grill to hot. Mix the custard with the crème fraîche. Put a shallow layer of fruit into individual gratin dishes, cover with the custard mixture and sprinkle with the sugar.

2 Pop under a hot grill until the sugar caramelizes, then serve.

Chilled apricot and rice pudding

Total preparation/cooking time: 30 minutes plus
    chilling
Serves 3–4

about 1 litre/1¾pts full cream milk
2 or 3 heaped tbsp rich honey
150g/5oz white pudding rice, rinsed and drained
50g/2oz dried apricots, chopped
4 green cardamom pods, crushed
2 tbsp mixed chopped unsalted nuts e.g. almonds,
    pistachios, cashews
2 tbsp caster sugar

1 Put the milk and the honey in a large pan and bring to the boil, whisking all the time to combine. Turn down the heat. Add everything else except the nuts and the sugar and simmer until you have a nice creamy rice pudding. Chill in the refrigerator.

2 Just before serving, dissolve the caster sugar in a pan and stir in the chopped nuts until they caramelize. Pour onto a piece of greaseproof paper to set. Once set, break them up and sprinkle over the chilled rice to serve.

Floyd's knickerbocker glory

A Spanish version of knickerbocker glory.

Total preparation time: 10 minutes

For each serving
1 tub of top-quality crème caramel from the supermarket
several scoops of ice cream in different flavours
lots of fresh fruit – for example, strawberries, pineapple,
    peaches, pears, banana
a whirl of fresh whipped cream
and, of course, a cherry for the top

1 Carefully remove the crème caramel from its mould
and put into the bottom of a tall glass, or on a serving
plate or into a bowl.

2 Cover with scoops of ice cream – whatever you like,
or whatever you have – chocolate, pistachio,
strawberry or vanilla. Pile on some fruit, smother with
cream and pop a cherry on top.

Floyd's knickerbocker glory - fruity
and cooling on a hot summer's day

Poached pears with mascarpone –
an impressive-looking dessert

Plantation banana custard

The reason for the bizarre title of this dish is that somewhere in Africa I found myself on a banana plantation and the only means of cooking this we had was over a fire in a hole in the ground, which at the time was huge fun, but it's also dead easy to do in the oven.

Total preparation/cooking time: 25 minutes
Serves 2

4 egg yolks
300ml/½pt double cream
dash of vanilla extract
2 bananas, sliced
soft brown sugar

1 Preheat the oven to 180°C/350°F, gas mark 4. Beat the egg yolks, then blend in the cream and add the vanilla extract. Lay the slices of banana in the bottom of a ramekin dish and pour the egg and cream mixture on top. Sprinkle liberally with the sugar and bake in the oven for about 20 minutes, or until the sugar has caramelized.

Poached pears with mascarpone

Total preparation/cooking time: 30 minutes
**   plus chilling**
Serves 6

6 medium pears, peeled with stems left on
2 heaped tbsp honey
juice and finely grated zest of 1 lemon
1 crushed vanilla pod
2 lightly crushed cardamom pods
large broken stick of cinnamon

For the mascarpone sauce
2 egg yolks
2 heaped tbsp honey
250g/9oz mascarpone cheese
grated nutmeg, to serve

1 Put the honey, lemon juice and zest, vanilla pod, cardamom pods and cinnamon into a pan, bring to the boil and continue boiling until the liquid is reduced by half. Turn down the heat, add the pears and simmer for about 15 minutes until they are soft, then chill.

2 To make the mascarpone, blend the eggs yolks with the honey, then blend in the mascarpone cheese and chill. Serve the pears with the mascarpone sauce and sprinkle on a little grated nugmeg.

You can also make this recipe with figs – use 8, cut in half.

Brochette of summer fruits with raspberry sauce

Total preparation/cooking time: 15 minutes plus marinating

Thread the fruits onto 20.5cm/8in skewers.

Per person
selection of fresh fruit, e.g. plums, apricots, strawberries, banana, pineapple, peaches, mango etc., all cut to the size of a strawberry
lemon juice
caster sugar
fresh unsalted pistachio nuts, chopped, to serve
clotted cream, to serve

For the raspberry sauce
generous punnet of raspberries
2 tbsp caster or icing sugar
juice of 1 lemon

1 Thread the fruit onto the skewers and marinate in the lemon juice for 15 minutes.

2 To make the raspberry sauce, simmer the ingredients gently over a low heat for a couple of minutes, then whiz in a food processor, strain and refrigerate.

3 Preheat the grill to its maximum, sprinkle the brochettes liberally with caster sugar and grill until the sugar is caramelised. Put a small dollop of raspberry sauce onto each plate and place the kebab on top. Mix the pistachio nuts into the clotted cream and serve with the brochettes.

Kiwi fruit sunset

Also known as Chinese gooseberries, kiwi fruit not only taste delicious when ripe, but they're full of vitamin C.

Total preparation/cooking time: 20 minutes plus chilling
Serves 4

4 large kiwi fruit, peeled and thinly sliced
110g/4oz caster sugar
2 whole cloves
7.5cm/3in cinnamon stick
270ml/9fl oz red wine
1 lime, cut into 8 thin slices

1 Put the sugar, spices and wine in a pan and pour in 270ml/9fl oz cold water. Bring to the boil, then simmer gently for 15 minutes. Allow to cool.

2 Place the fruit in the wine sauce and chill before serving.

Rice fritters

If, like me, you find yourself stuck with some cooked rice from your last Indian takeaway, or you buy a tub of cooked rice from the supermarket, then you have all it needs to make an instant pudding!

Total preparation/cooking time: 15 minutes
Makes about 20

175g/6oz short-grain (pudding) rice, cooked
50g/2oz plain flour
1 tsp baking powder
pinch of salt
2 eggs, beaten
½ tsp vanilla essence
4 tbsp desiccated coconut
3 tbsp caster sugar
vegetable oil, for deep-frying
icing sugar, for dusting

1 Sift together the flour, baking powder and salt into a large bowl, then whisk in the eggs and vanilla essence. Stir in the cooked rice, coconut and sugar to make a thick batter.

2 Heat the oil in a deep-fat fryer to 180°C/350°F – test by popping in a cube of bread to see if it sizzles. Deep-fry tablespoonfuls of the mixture in the hot fat, one at a time, until golden-brown. Drain on kitchen paper, then dust with icing sugar. Serve immediately.

Zabaglione

For a frothy dessert or, indeed, a pick-me-up for those under the weather, whisk Marsala with egg yolks and sugar and you have Zabaglione! This is simple to make but quite hard work. Your whisking hand needs to be in good shape.

Total preparation/cooking time: 10 minutes

Per person
2 large egg yolks
2 tbsp caster sugar
a dash of Marsala

1 Whisk together the egg yolks and sugar, then put the mixing bowl over a pan of gently simmering water. Pour in the alcohol and whisk madly until you have a smooth, frothy, thick, custard-like mixture. Serve in glasses with sweet biscuits.

Sydney sunrise

This is one of the best hangover cures in the world. Sometime back, I was helming an ex-America's Cup yacht, in Sydney harbour. It was very early in the morning and I was feeling a bit groggy until the skipper offered me this refreshing heart-starting drink. Put the following things in the blender:

Total preparation time: 5 minutes
Serves 2

2 tbsp runny honey, juice of 4 oranges, juice of 2 limes, ¼ tsp powdered cinnamon and 2 whole fresh eggs. Whiz the lot until you have a frothy, creamy drink. Pour into tall glasses filled with ice, and recover.

Dougal's dollop!

While filming in Benidorm, I spent a terrific morning in a pub called the Magic Roundabout, a haven for Brits, because it pays lip-service to Spanish food but really comes on strong with steak and kidney pies and all those good British favourites. They also had rugby on satellite television so that in between takes I was able to sit and watch the games. And while I was watching and chatting to the manager Terry Williams we drank this rather innocuous-sounding but lethal drinkette.

Total preparation time: 5 minutes
Makes about 1 litre/1¾ pts

1 Make this potent little number by putting a couple of handfuls of ice into as large a jug as you can find. Pour over plenty of fresh orange juice and then add the bottle of bubbly. Let the fizz subside a bit, then add the magic ingredient – Cointreau. Now I know how the pub where we tried this, the Magic Roundabout, got its name.

Sydney sunrise - one of the best
hangover cures in the world

Sangria

There are many variations but the basic recipe is made with red wine, brandy, cinnamon, bits of fruit and some fizz (for example, fizzy orange, lemon or soda). If you want to make it stronger, add more hard alcohol. Make sure it is served icy cold - allow plenty of time for it to chill in the refrigerator.

Total preparation time: 5 minutes plus chilling
Makes about 1 litre/1¾ pts

1 apple, diced
1 pear, diced
1 orange, thinly sliced
1 lemon, thinly sliced
Cointreau
brandy
banana liqueur
1 bottle of dry, full-bodied red wine
1 small bottle of fizzy orange, chilled
1 small bottle of fizzy lemon, chilled
1 tsp sugar
1 cinnamon stick
ice cubes

1 Put the apple, pear, orange and lemon slices into as large a jug as you can find. Then add a generous amount of the Cointreau, brandy and banana liqueur. Pour in the bottle of wine and leave to chill thoroughly. When the drink is really cold, pour in the fizzy orange and lemon and add the sugar and cinnamon stick. Throw in a few ice cubes, pour into some glasses and drink it.

Fire and ice

While I was filming in India, Pritam, the excellent bartender of the Trident Hotel in Udaipur, made this refreshing drink for me.

Total preparation time: 5 minutes
Serves 1

1 tbsp fresh lime juice
2 tbsp sugar syrup (see page 139)
1 tsp very, very finely chopped deseeded green chilli
1 tsp very, very finely chopped fresh mint
1 tbsp or so crushed ice
200 ml/7 fl oz fresh pineapple juice

For the garnish
1 lime slice
1 fresh mint leaf

1 Put the lime juice, sugar syrup, green chilli, mint and ice into a suitable glass. Top up with the pineapple juice and stir well. Serve garnished with a lime slice and a mint leaf. Delicious!

Note
You could, of course, reduce the quantity of fresh pineapple juice and substitute the difference with vodka. Or to hell with it. Why substitute the pineapple juice? Just slosh in the vodka.

Sangria - make
sure it's served
icy cold

Tinto verano

This literally means 'summer red wine'. It is the great southern Spanish drink, not to be confused with sangria, and not to be dismissed because it sounds common! If you want to enjoy your lunch on the beach under the Andalusian sun you don't want to mess about with expensive bottles of Rioja or high-alcohol cocktails like sangria. Take a large tumbler, quarter fill it with ice and squeeze in the lime juice. Fill the glass to two-thirds with red wine and stir in some lemonade.

Total preparation time: 5 minutes
Per person

Mango delight

A really refreshing summer cocktail that will, in fact, work with any soft, ripe fruit. For one person take the chopped-up flesh of a large ripe mango, a couple of ice cubes, the juice of one fresh lime, a dash of coconut milk, a large dash of white rum and a dash of cane sugar syrup. Whack the lot into a blender and whiz. You can, of course, decorate it with exotic fruit if you want.

Total preparation time: 5 minutes
Per person

Fruit lassi

Purée any soft fruit of your choice, such as raspberries, strawberries, mangoes, apricots or bananas, obviously husked or peeled. Then chuck in a couple of ice cubes, some sugar syrup and some natural yoghurt and whiz until you have a creamy milkshake-type drink. You can buy sugar syrup, known as Syrop de Canne, in any decent wine store. Or use my recipe below.

Total preparation time: 12 minutes
Per person

Sugar syrup

1 To make sugar syrup, put 50g/2oz sugar (granulated or caster) in a saucepan with 300ml/$\frac{1}{2}$pt water. Place over a moderate heat and stir until the sugar has dissolved. Bring to the boil and simmer for 3 or 4 minutes, then remove from the heat. Leave to cool. The syrup can be stored in the fridge for several weeks.

Index